Kitchen Witchcraft Crystal Magic

The third book in the Kitchen Witchcraft series following on from Spells & Charms and Garden Magic

Kitchen Witchcraft Crystal Magic

The third book in the Kitchen Witchcraft series following on from Spells & Charms and Garden Magic

Rachel Patterson

MOON BOOKS

Winchester, UK
Washington, USA

JOHN HUNT PUBLISHING

First published by Moon Books, 2019
Moon Books is an imprint of John Hunt Publishing Ltd., No. 3 East Street, Alresford
Hampshire SO24 9EE, UK
office@jhpbooks.net
www.johnhuntpublishing.com
www.moon-books.net

For distributor details and how to order please visit the 'Ordering' section on our website.

Text copyright: Rachel Patterson 2018

ISBN: 978 1 78904 216 0
978 1 78904 217 7 (ebook)
Library of Congress Control Number: 2018961985

A CIP catalogue record for this book is available from the British Library.

Design: Stuart Davies

UK: Printed and bound by CPI Group (UK) Ltd, Croydon, CR0 4YY
US: Printed and bound by Thomson-Shore, 7300 West Joy Road, Dexter, MI 48130

We operate a distinctive and ethical publishing philosophy in
all areas of our business, from our global network of authors to
production and worldwide distribution.

Contents

Who am I?

I am a witch ... have been for a very long time. I am also a working wife and mother who has also been lucky enough to write and have published a book or fifteen. I love to learn, I love to study and have done so from books, online resources, schools and wonderful mentors over the years and continue to learn every day but have learnt the most from getting outside and doing it.

I like to laugh, bake and eat cake...

I am High Priestess of the Kitchen Witch Coven and an Elder at the online Kitchen Witch School.

I also have regular blogs on:
Witches & Pagans - www.witchesandpagans.com/pagan-paths-blogs/hedge-witch.html
Patheos Pagan - www.patheos.com/blogs/beneaththemoon
Moon Books – www.moon-books.net/blogs/moonbooks/author/rachelp
Wyldwood – www.wyldwood.org

My website and personal blog: www.rachelpatterson.co.uk
Facebook: www.facebook.com/rachelpattersonbooks
Email: kitchenwitchhearth@yahoo.com

Kitchen Witch School website and blog:
www.kitchenwitchhearth.net
www.facebook.com/kitchenwitchuk

My craft is a combination of old religion Witchcraft, Kitchen Witchery, Hedge Witchery and folk magic. My heart is that of a Kitchen Witch.

CRYSTAL MAGIC

Where do crystals come from?

'Crystals' is a blanket title that covers all sorts of stones, minerals and metals and they can be found all around us. From the sand between our toes on the beach to huge marble statues and concrete buildings and of course all the semi-precious and precious stones in between.

All of these come from the earth, they are collected from rivers and sea shores and mined from hills, caves and mountains.

What we see as the end product has actually taken millions of years to create.

Earth is made from layers which are continuously moving, not so we would notice though, well not all the time. Stresses can fracture the layers, and this is where crystals can form. Hot liquids and gases from below the earth force their way up towards the surface bringing with them molten rock which is called magma. All of this gets other elements and compounds thrown at it such as sodium, iron, water and oxygen. As they pass through the less active and much cooler layers of the earth the elements fall out of solution and start to crystallise in any crevice they can find. What crystal forms will depend on which elements are present and the conditions of the environment at that time and place. This is how a lot of the harder precious gemstones such as rubies and diamonds are formed.

As the crust of Earth moves and changes the conditions alter and you get different waves of crystallisation. The rocks and minerals are changed into new compositions by this continuous movement, this is called metamorphic. The metamorphic rocks and crystals are surrounded by pressure and heat. As soon as the Earth moves enough to allow water and ice in, the rocks start to erode. Rock particles are washed away, settling in riverbanks or the sea. Millions of years later after deposits have built up, the weight and the water above them compresses to form sedimentary rock. It is within sedimentary rock that we find the less hard crystals.

The colour of any crystal is determined by the different elements that create impurities within its structure.

Did you get all that? There will be a test...

Ethics

The basic fact is that crystals are taken from Mother Earth and some of the mining practices can be extremely harsh to the environment. Only you can make the decision about where you source your crystals from. There are some very good eco-friendly crystal providers, it may just take a bit of research on your part. A lot of crystal suppliers are now stating their sources which is very helpful. If you are interested in working with natural items for magical purpose you may want to take a peek at one of my other books, Witchcraft into the Wilds (total and absolutely unashamed book plug).

The power within

How does a crystal or stone have magical powers? I believe that every natural item has energy, some call it an energy field, others may refer to it as an aura. Whatever name you give it, the energy has power that you can tap into. Crystals in particular have a structure that allows them to receive, collect, store and project energy. Don't take my word for it, those clever science bods have apparently done all kinds of tests to confirm that this actually happens. Think of crystals and stones as natural batteries.

Each individual crystal or stone will have a very unique character and energy. You may connect with them or not, it will depend on how compatible your energy field is with that of the crystal. Just as you find you get on with some humans and not others. No two crystals will have the same energy. Even if you get two crystals of the same type, they will have a different feel from each other. Some crystals will have stronger energy than others, it isn't always dependent on size either.

I often find that something like rose quartz has a soft and gentle vibe, but a crystal such as hematite is a lot stronger and heavier. But that's just my perspective, you may find it otherwise!

The use of crystals as charms and jewellery dates back for thousands of years (those clever ancient Egyptians were using them as far back as 1500BC). Some of the rarest and most expensive precious stones carry curses or chequered histories with them. Perhaps this shows that stones which have been stolen or gained through foul play hold onto huge amounts of negative energy?

Whether you choose to place them around your home, wear them as amulets and talismans, use them for divination or work healing and magic with them, it is definitely an interesting journey.

Categories

The term 'crystals' is used to cover a huge array of items; precious gems, semi-precious gems, crystals and stones. I love to work with natural stones and pebbles and they are of course the easiest to find and as an added bonus they are free. A pebble from the sea shore and a diamond have very similar structures just with different elements, the diamond has the added ingredient of carbon. Rocks and stones are natural solid mineral grains and/ or glass whereas crystals are classified because of the way they hold and reflect the light.

The difference between precious and semi-precious gems is the price...and that is because the precious (i.e. expensive) ones are rarer. Diamonds, emeralds, rubies and sapphires are precious whereas gems such as amethyst and quartz are semi-precious. Gems are rated as such because of their quality, beauty, colour and hardness.

Choosing

If you are lucky enough to have a decent crystal store nearby then choosing the crystal yourself (or letting it choose you, as that seems to be the usual way) is good. But not everyone has access to hands on crystal shops, so purchasing from a reputable online source is absolutely fine. Don't forget to look about in your local area; on the beach, river banks, woodlands or forests can all be sources of natural stones and pebbles. Check out charity/thrift stores too as crystals sometimes find their way to them too. You don't have to spend a fortune, although it is tempting. Start small and with the basics. Beautiful magic can be worked with a pebble or a shell. The rough unpolished crystals are usually cheaper than the cut and prettied up ones and the energy will be the same either way, in fact I often prefer the raw unpolished stones myself.

Trust your intuition and pick a stone that resonates with you. If you are in a store hold your hand above the crystals and see if you can feel any heat or energy. If you are shopping online see what images jump out at you. Go in with an open mind, don't be too set on a particular stone. I have discovered that the right stones will find you. In my experience crystals sometimes arrive from friends as gifts and you will occasionally feel the need to pass one or two of your own on to someone else. Crystals know when their work is done or if they need to move on...go with the flow.

If you are looking for a crystal to work magic with for a specific intent, get the idea, the goal or the desired outcome set in your mind and then ask yourself what crystal you need to use. Hopefully either the name or the colour of a crystal will pop right into your head. If it doesn't, have a look through the crystals you have and see which one jumps out at you. Hold it in your hand and ask if it is the right one to work with, you should get a positive or a negative feeling.

Cleansing

Once you get the crystal home and in your sticky little paw you may want to cleanse it. You don't know how many other people have handled the stone, including snotty little children (or snotty adults) ...each one will have left their own personal energy on the crystal. A crystal will also need cleansing after it has been used for spell working or healing. If it has been left on a shelf or in a box for a long while it will probably benefit from a 'once over' as well.

Go with what supplies you have to hand, or what works for you when cleansing a crystal. But do check first, some stones are porous or fade in sunlight. Trust your intuition on this, you may 'feel' that each crystal needs a specific method of cleansing. I think it helps to cleanse and charge crystals in a way that matches their energy.

My cleansing suggestions:

Visualisation: Cheapest and simplest option. Visualise a white light coming from the sun, the moon or the sky and direct it into the crystal. See it cleansing and purifying any negative energy away.

Water: Run your crystal under the tap or drop it into a bowl of water. Allow the water to wash away any negative energy.

Incense: Light an incense of your choice and waft it over the crystal or holding the crystal in your hand move it through the smoke.

Sun: Leave your crystal in the sunlight, either outside if it is safe or on a windowsill for an hour or two – until you feel it is cleansed.

Moon: Leave your crystal in the moonlight, either outside if it is safe or on a windowsill for an hour or two – until you feel it is cleansed. This is best done under a full moon but work with the moon phases dependent on whether you want to work drawing magic (money, prosperity, love etc.) which would benefit from charging under waxing moon. Crystals that you intend to work releasing magic with would be better charged under a waning moon.

Earth: Bury your stone in the soil for a few hours. Probably best done in a flower pot otherwise you might forget where you buried it...

Air: Hold the crystal in your hand and using your breath, blow on it, turning the crystal around until you have literally blown away all the negative energy.

Sound: Place your crystal down and drum around it or use a singing bowl, cymbals or any kind of musical instrument of your choice.

Rice: Bury the crystal into a bowl of dried (uncooked) rice and leave for a few hours.

Fire: You need to be careful with this one. Light a candle and pass the crystal just above the flame to cleanse.

Other crystals: Some crystals are natural cleansers. Lay your crystal that needs clearing on top of a larger quartz or amethyst cluster.

Herbs: Sprinkle a blend of herbs and/or petals over the crystal or pop them in a pouch or jar that is filled with herbs and plant matter.

Crystals under the full moon

Social media is full of memes advising everyone to pop their crystals out to cleanse, purify and soak up the moonlight on a full moon...but I don't...and it isn't because I don't like being told what to do...

I do put some crystals out on the full moon but not all of them. There are some crystals that I think suit the moonlight but others that I find work better by being put out in either the sunshine or even the rain and wind.

For instance I put stones like moonstone (obviously!), quartz and blue lace agate out in the moonlight.

But for stones such as sunstone, topaz, tiger's eye, carnelian, amber and all the fiery stones I like to put them in the sunshine so that they soak up the masculine energy instead.

And then we have watery stones, if it is raining then there are some stones that love being out in it such as amethyst, blue lace agate and lapis. (Note: don't put porous stones out in the rain… they may not be there when you get back…).

You can even take it further and separate them into the four elements and put out air stones on a windy day and bury earth stones (carefully and mark where you put them) in the soil.

Air stones would be things like amethyst, citrine and turquoise. For earth these stones might be agate, jasper and jet.

Obviously some of the stones will fit into a couple of the categories and I also go by colour; yellow, red and orange stones go in the sun and white, blue and pale stones go under the moon.

Trust your intuition…but I prefer not to lump all the stones under the moon because it is incredibly powerful and I personally feel that some of my crystals work better with sun, wind or water energy instead.

Go with what feels right for you…

Connecting and energy

Before you work with any crystal I recommend connecting with the energy it contains.

Every natural item has its own energy field and it is just a matter of tapping into that to find out what specific help it can provide to you.

Sit quietly and hold the crystal in your hands. Open your mind and reach out with your spidery senses and connect with the aura/energy field of the crystal. Ask it what it can help you with.

Carry the crystal with you and/or sleep with it under your pillow – this will help you connect to the crystal and it will also help make the link with your energy.

Some crystals will have stronger energy than others, it will depend on the size of the crystal, type of crystal and also whether it is compatible with you. You may find that there are some crystals that totally resonate with you, others you may distinctly not like, you may even find it uncomfortable to hold them.

Meditation

I also recommend meditating with any new crystal you acquire. Sit quietly and put the crystal down in front of you. Clear your mind and allow your focus to be directed at the crystal. See it, really see it in great detail. What colours do you see? What inclusions, cracks, lines or spots do you see on the surface? What about under the surface? Really delve deep into the stone. Explore...

Crystals can be used as a focal point for meditation or as an aid to help you on your meditation journey.

Holding the crystal in your hand or creating a meditation journey pouch that holds crystals works well but you can also lie or sit with crystals placed on your body. This works particularly well if you are laying down as you can place a crystal on your third eye, it will help you reach a meditative state and amplify your insight.

Crystal meditation

Find a comfortable place where you won't be disturbed. Put on some plinky plonky music if it helps you meditate and light some incense if you would like to.

Hold your crystal in the palm of both hands. Sit and look at the crystal, turn it around and upside down. Really see all the tiny details, the shape, the colours and the landscape of it.

Now either close your eyes and visualise the crystal in your mind's eye or keep your eyes open and focus on the crystal you are holding.

Allow yourself to travel down into the crystal (or visualise the crystal growing larger, big enough for you to explore). See yourself walking over the outside of the crystal, investigating any cracks or chips within.

Feel the energy of the crystal, talk to it, make a connection with it. Take your time to explore...

Ask the crystal what magic it can help you with.

And when you are ready slowly and gently come back to this reality. Wriggle your fingers and ground yourself.

Programming and charging

When you want to work with a crystal within magic you will need to charge it with the energy of your intent. Basically, you need to tell it what you would like it to do. Do be polite and ask it nicely but make sure you really push that energy. The strength of your will and commitment to the outcome is paramount in any spell work. That crystal needs to be very, very clear about what you expect from it and what you would like it to do.

You can add to the programming by doing one, some or all of the following:

Visualise your intent and send that image into the stone.

Set up a candle in a corresponding colour and maybe even inscribe a symbol into the candle or sprinkle it with herbs and oils. Place the crystal in front of the lit candle and allow the energy to be soaked up into the stone.

Place the crystal in a pouch for a while and add dried herbs that correspond to your intent. Let the crystal fill up with the energy from the herbs.

Light some incense and pass the crystal through the smoke, whilst telling the crystal what you need from it.

Create a gemstone altar (see chapter on crystal altars) and place the crystal on it to charge.

The aftermath

Once you have finished working magic with a crystal you can re-use it, but I would suggest cleansing it first (using one of the methods above). If you don't it will carry the energy from the last spell and could confuse the issue if you use it next time for another purpose.

Remember that crystals store energy, positive or negative. It is really important to release any negative thoughts or feelings before you work with crystals. Any stray negative vibes that are floating around within you may get transferred inadvertently into the crystal when you are working with it. The crystal will then hold onto those bad vibes. If you are charging crystals with visualisation, make sure you do so on a day when you are feeling happy and positive. Be careful where you send that negative nonsense! It is particularly important to cleanse crystals if you have used them for healing, they may have absorbed some of the illness nasties and you don't want to transfer that to anyone else.

Inclusions

Not all crystals will be clear or pure, a lot of them will have what are called inclusions. I love crystals that have these as I think it makes them far more interesting to work with. Basically, it is an imperfect within the stone. It is caused by material being trapped inside the crystal as it grew. It might be a different mineral, but it could also have been liquid, gas/vapour or even in some cases small insects or plant matter.

Projection and reception

Some stones are better at projective energy and others suited to reception. Think male and female, sun and moon, ying and yang, hot and cold or day and night. It does seem that the brighter sunshiny coloured stones are more on the projective power side of things with the lighter blues and greens being receptive. But again, trust how you feel about a particular stone, they are all individual.

Projective stones will often feel very energetic to the touch, sometimes literally fizzing with energy. Projective crystals are good for protection and healing along with anything of the positive body and mind image magics such as confidence and strength. Receptive stones will usually give a soft calm energy out and sometimes feel cold to the touch. Receptive stones are good for emotional issues, spiritual and psychic magic and for calm and peace. Obviously not every stone will fall exactly on either side of the fence and some will be total rebels and climb the fence to the other side. Something like quartz will sit on top of the fence as it works as a multi-purpose stone. Black stones for example like to buck the trend and will fall on either side depending on their type. Hold the stone and connect with the energy, you will soon become accustomed to what type of energy it is and how it can help you.

Life is all about balance and crystals can be used to help create that wonderful situation of equilibrium. If you find yourself feeling angry or irritable then you may have way too much projective energy floating around your body, work with a receptive crystal to balance it out. And conversely if you are feeling moody and emotional you may be overflowing with receptive energy, work with a projection crystal to bring about the balance.

Projective:	Receptive:
Hot	Cold
Summer	Winter
Active	Inert
Yang	Ying
Male	Female
Outward	Inward
Sun	Moon

11

Day	Night
Fire	Water
Air	Earth
Physical	Spiritual
Light	Dark
God	Goddess

Work Magic with Projective stones for:
Strength
Healing
Protection
Vitality
Courage
Power
Determination
Will power
Self confidence
Luck
Success

Some examples of projective stones are:
Bloodstone, carnelian, citrine, garnet, red jasper, rhodocrosite, tiger's eye

Work magic with receptive stones for:
Calming
Spirituality
Meditation
Emotions
Grounding
Psychic abilities
The subconscious
Love

Compassion
Peace
Wisdom
Communication

Some examples of receptive stones are:
Hag stones, jade, kunzite, lapis lazuli, malachite, moonstone, pink tourmaline, rose quartz, sugilite and turquoise

Magical bling

I do like a bit of crystal bling whether in the form of bracelets, pendants, earrings or rings and I even have a brooch or two. The metal that the item is made from carries magical energy and so does any stones that are set into it. They have their own individual magical properties but can also be charged with a specific intent to become an amulet or a talisman.

Amulets and Talismans: Tying a spell into a piece of jewellery or crystal. There is always confusion over the meaning for each of these, believe me I get confused too. It is all about attracting and deflecting...

Talisman – a magically charged object that ATTRACTS a desired energy. Talismans bring power and energy to the wearer. They can be made of anything from natural objects to pieces of parchment inscribed with symbols. You may have a piece of jewellery or an item of clothing which you wear to give you confidence or for luck, this is a talisman.

Amulet – a magically charged object which DEFLECTS unwanted energy. Amulets have been used for protection for thousands of years to protect people's homes, crops and livestock. Originally, they would probably have been made using natural objects like stones, animal bones and teeth. Now we can use all sorts of different materials and items. Even a knot in a piece of string could be used as an amulet as the knot will trap the unwanted energy and keep us safe.

If you are creating a talisman for luck you could create it during a waxing moon to enhance the attraction magic, you might use the colour green if you see that as a lucky colour. If it is a natural object like a pebble you might want to draw a four-leaf clover or a similar symbol on it. You get the idea, layer your correspondences to make it as meaningful as possible.

The same rules apply to an amulet; you would create this on a waning moon if possible. Your amulet maybe a black gemstone for protection and you might burn sage to cleanse negative energies and put it through the flame of a black candle during its creation.

You will need to charge both the talisman and the amulet with your intent.

Which crystal or jewellery item you choose to wear will be up to you. I like to be guided by my intuition as to what stone, design or colour. Often, I realise after I have purchased an item that the correspondences to that particular crystal are perfect for what I needed at the time. Crystals will often find their way to you, rather than you choosing them.

I might pick up a lapis lazuli pendant to wear because it matches my outfit but as soon as I pick it up it feels wrong. Searching through I will spy a rose quartz pendant and although it isn't the same colour as my dress it feels right to wear it – trust your instincts.

If you purchase a piece of jewellery for a specific intent, you can choose it by looking up the correspondences, working with colour magic or by intuition (or a combination of all three). You can then add to the magical intent by charging the item. This can be done via the means above in the 'charging' section. For jewellery it can also be put on your altar for a few days or worked into a candle magic spell set for the intent.

And how about where on your body to wear the item? The left side of the body is your emotional side full of sensitive feelings and then the right side is your go get 'em action energy.

The type of jewellery can be taken into account as well.

Earrings can be worn to protect against headaches and anything to do with healing and protecting your eyes, ears and brain.

Necklaces involve a chain or string of some sort, so they carry binding or linking magic. They also go around the throat and neck/chest area so can be used to help free speech and matters of the heart. **Bracelets** are a smaller version of binding/linking magic and as they are around the wrists I think they work well for creativity and getting things done. Bracelets also cover the pulse points on your wrist, so any crystals worn will connect directly with your internal energy hub.

Rings are circles so they represent eternity and infinity. Your fingers also have associations; index finger for goals and success, middle finger for intuition and inspiration, ring finger for creativity and on your left hand, love and the little finger for transitions and change. And your thumb should probably be avoided as wearing rings on your thumb can block the flow of energy.

Anklets being worn around the ankle help you connect with the earth and can bring stability and be very grounding.

Brooches were all the rage in my favourite era (the mid-1980s) and I still wear them now (never having left 1984 really). They can be worn for protection, think of them as little shields.

Headdresses – most people don't pop down to the supermarket wearing a tiara but if you wear a headdress in ritual or for working magic think about adding a crystal or two. A headdress connects with your third eye and crown chakra brining intuition, energy and knowledge.

Wearing crystal jewellery brings magic into play without anyone noticing, much easier to wear a crystal pendant than have several tumble stones tucked into your bra or vest!

Crystal arguments

I have mentioned that not everyone will connect with all the crystals, it really is a personal energy interaction thing. But some crystals also don't work well together. Either their energy fights or they cancel each other out. It doesn't cause a huge crystal punch up or anything so dramatic but it could cause confusion in the intent or just cancel out the energy, which is a bit of a waste of time. Trust your intuition as always and if you put a pairing together and the energy feels wrong, swap one of them out.

Here are some traditional argumentative crystal pairings:
Lapis lazuli cancels out blue lace agate.
Lapis lazuli and turquoise are also complete enemies.
Carnelian negates any actions amethyst puts into play.
Carnelian cancels out blue lace agate.
Turquoise completely bullies and overpowers malachite.

Shape matters

If you already have a collection of crystals, then you will probably note they are all different shapes and sizes. Tumbled stones are smooth and small, clusters are sharp and look like something from a Star Trek set and rough pieces come in all shapes and sizes. Most of them are usually non-descript in shape but you sometimes find stones that are in specific shapes and each one has an added meaning, but more importantly what does the shape mean to you?

Clusters – a recognised and common form of crystals, these will bring balance and harmony. A lot of clusters are also used for cleansing and purifying whether it is your home or other crystals placed on them.

Obelisks/long – often quartz but lots of crystals can be obtained in this shape and they work well as wands to activate and manifest. And of course, the very shape of them is ahem... well masculine. They have power, energy, love and the ability to project.

Round – these reflect the world and indeed the universe, infinity, fertility, healing, spirituality, psychic abilities, attraction, manifestation, connection and the Goddess, they also bring a feminine energy and work well in love magic.

Triangle – a good shaped stone for protection.

Square – as the round is feminine so the square is masculine (hey I don't make the rules), square stones represent the God and bring power, energy and protection. They work well in sex and love magical workings. They also carry an earthy energy bringing prosperity and abundance along with stability and grounding.

Pyramid – excellent for healing, prosperity and manifestation.

Diamond – as the name suggests, any diamond shaped stone brings wealth, riches and prosperity.

L shape – bringing luck and good fortune.

Egg – an egg-shaped crystal will add the magic of fertility, creativity, new beginnings and ideas.

Heart – possibly an obvious one...heart shaped crystals bring love, romance, chocolates and flowers.

Size doesn't matter

We have all seen images on social media of enormous crystal formations (often amethyst or quartz), so large that they dwarf the person standing next to it. And much as it would probably be very nice to own a piece that large, first of all where would you put it? And secondly who could afford it? I have a few larger pieces of crystal (the size of my palm), most of them I have been lucky enough to find in charity/thrift stores. If I had a few hundred pounds going spare (laughs hysterically...coz that never happens) then I am not sure I could bring myself to spend it on a lump of rock, sparkly as it may be. I also think that huge pieces of crystal aren't necessary for working magic and would probably overpower a lot of things anyway. Like using a chainsaw to cut your toenails, too much overkill! I prefer to work with tumble stones. They are usually cheap and very easy to work with. You get the power you need to work magic and they fit neatly into spell pouches or witch bottles. They are also inexpensive enough to get a selection to work amazing crystal grids with.

Colour magic

I love to work with colour magic and that goes for crystals too. Often when I am working with a spell I will pick the crystals to use purely by their colour. In fact, I keep all my crystals in boxes, sorted into colours. Colour has such a big impact on how we feel, and I think it is important to incorporate into spell work.

Go with your intuition on this, you may associate different colours with the intents than I do, but here is a basic guide:

Black stones – receptive and associated with Saturn and the element of earth.

Useful for these magical workings – Stability, grounding, invisibility, protection, ward negativity, remove hexes, spirit contact, truth, binding and to remove discord or confusion.

Blue stones – receptive and associated with Neptune and the element of water.

Useful for these magical workings – Peace, the Goddess, water elemental, truth, dreams, protection, change, meditation, healing, psychic awareness, intuition, opportunity, understanding, safe journey, patience, tranquillity, ward depression, emotions, sleep, purification, healing and health.

Brown stones – receptive and associated with the element of earth.

Useful for these magical workings - Endurance, houses & homes, uncertainties, influence friendships.

Green stones – receptive and associated with Venus and the element of earth.

Useful for these magical workings - earth elemental, nature and garden magic, luck, fertility, healing, health, balance, courage, work, prosperity, money, grounding, balance, changing directions or attitudes.

Orange stones – projective and associated with the sun.

Useful for these magical workings: The God, strength, healing, attraction/manifestation, vitality, adaptability, luck, self-esteem, self-worth encouragement, clearing the mind, justice, career goals, protection, illumination, personal power, legal matters, selling, action, ambition, general success.

Pink stones – receptive and associated with Venus.

Useful for these magical workings – honour, morality, friendships, emotional love, social ability, good will, caring, healing emotions, peace, affection, nurturing, self-love, happiness, openness, romance and partnerships.

Purple stones – receptive and associated with Jupiter and Neptune.

Useful for these magical workings – Mysticism, power, spirit, spiritual development, intuition, ambition, healing, wisdom, progress, business, purification, spirit communication, protection, occultism, self-assurance, meditation, spirit communication, karma workings, neutralize baneful magic, spiritual development, peace, psychic growth, divination, Otherworld.

Red stones – projective and associated with Mars and the element of fire.

Useful for these magical workings: fire elemental, strength, power, energy, health, vigour, death and rebirth, protection, blood healing and magic, sex magic, enthusiasm, courage, passion, sexuality, vibrancy, survival, driving force.

White stones – receptive and associated with the Moon.

Useful for these magical workings: Sleep, psychic abilities, luck, fortune, purity, protection, truth, meditation, peace, sincerity, justice and to ward doubt and fear.

Yellow stones – projective and associated with Mercury and the Sun.

Useful for these magical workings: Communication, air elemental, divination, protection, visualisation, clairvoyance, mental alertness, intellect, memory, prosperity, learning, changes, harmony, creativity, movement, change, self-promotion.

Multi-coloured stones – for stones that contain two or more colours then they often combine the magical properties of each colour.

Absorbing crystal colours

Colour magic is a powerful tool and working with a crystal to absorb its 'colour energy' is magical and can help lift your mood, ease pain or calm you down. Take a look at the colour magic correspondences and see which colour you feel you need to absorb. A yellow crystal might make you feel happy if you are sad, a blue crystal could help with healing and a green crystal may calm you down if you are feeling angry.

There are several ways to do this:

Carry a crystal with you or wear it as a piece of jewellery.

Put a crystal under your pillow.

Soak a crystal in a glass of spring water, then drink the water (take the crystal out first) or splash the water on your pulse points – Note: please check that the crystal is the type that does not leech bits into the water!

Add crystals to your bath.

Sit inside a circle of crystals for a while.

Chakras

Extending from colour magic you can work with crystals to cleanse and clear your chakras, assigning a different crystal to each one of your chakras, usually the associated colour. Lay down and place them on each chakra (or get someone else to place them as it is quite tricky doing it yourself when you are lying flat on the floor). Then allow the crystals to work their magic.

The basic nine chakras and suggested crystals to use are:

Soul star – white – quartz, selenite

Crown – violet – amethyst, quartz

Third eye – indigo – lapis lazuli, fluorite

Throat – blue – blue lace agate, tiger's eye

Heart – green, pink – rose quartz, aventurine

Solar plexus – yellow – citrine, topaz

Sacral – orange – carnelian, amber

Root/base – red - carnelian

Earth star – brown – smoky quartz, obsidian

Witch bottles

I have written about these before, but crystals work really well in them.

I love using witch bottles, I always have two on the go in my house for protection, clearing out negative energies and bringing happiness to the home. These are so easy to make, you don't need special pretty bottles you can just use old, clean jam jars.

In general terms, the witch bottles we make today are very similar to witch bottles found centuries ago, the structure is the same, but the intent differs quite a lot. Originally it was believed witch bottles were created to protect against witches... They also used to contain all sorts of bodily fluids, hair and finger nail clippings – you can still use these if you wish.

Basically, a witch bottle is a container of some sort, usually a jar or a bottle, which is filled with objects corresponding with and charged with a specific magical intent.

The typical contents of the basic protective witch bottle today are quite similar to that of the traditional one: Nails, sand, crystals, stones, knotted threads, herbs, spices, resin, flowers, candle wax, incense, salt, vinegar, oil, coins, saw dust, ashes etc. etc. Everything used in a standard spell can be used in this bottled version.

Start with your jar or bottle, then charge each item before you add it, layering up the 'ingredients' as you go.

It really is up to you what you put in. I like to put in three nails to draw any negative energy out of the house and into the bottle and for protection. I also put in a piece of string with three knots in, knotting in my intent with each tie. If it is for prosperity I often drop in a silver coin. I usually put salt in for protection, cleansing and purification. I also like to add a variety of dried pulse – lentils or beans to 'soak' up any negative energies. Garlic is good for protection too. Then add any herbs, spices and flowers that correspond with your intent – rose petals for love, cinnamon for success, mint and basil for prosperity etc. And of course, drop in a crystal that corresponds with your intent; hematite or obsidian are good for protection, tiger's eye is good for protection and prosperity, citrine for a happy home and rose quartz for love.

Keep filling the jar or bottle up until you reach the top then put the lid on. If you are using a jam jar I like to draw a pentacle on the lid. If I am using a bottle with a cork I like to seal the cork lid with dripped wax, not for any other reason except that it looks fabulous...

If you are making the witch bottle for protection for your own home I like to put in a pebble from the garden, a couple of fallen leaves from the tree in my yard and a bit of cobweb from inside the house, it makes it all more personal and ties the bottle to the energies of the home.

Poppets

When most people think of a poppet, they automatically think of the Voodoo doll, thanks to this item's negative portrayal in movies and on television. However, the use of dolls in sympathetic magic goes back several millennia. Back in the days of ancient Egypt, the enemies of Ramses III (he had a lot) used wax images of the Pharaoh, to bring about his death. Greek poppets called Kolossoi were sometimes used to restrain a ghost or even a dangerous deity, or to bind two lovers together.

I like to think of a poppet as a person shaped spell holder and use them for love, luck, protection, prosperity and healing.

Remember that poppets have a long tradition behind them, and that tradition is influenced by the magical practices of a wide range of cultures. Treat your poppets well, and they will do the same for you.

As for design, well it's up to you. You can make a simple poppet from twine, grasses or ivy tied together right up to detailed material poppets with hair and glass eyes and of course anywhere in between. You can even use dollies, Barbie dolls or a potato.

I like to use felt when making poppets because I hate sewing. With felt you don't have to hem. And of course, felt comes in all sorts of colours so you can correspond the colour of felt used to the intent.

I cut out two felt shapes, a bit like a gingerbread man or a 'T' shape. Then I sew one button on for one eye and a cross for the other eye, followed by a mouth. Then I sew on a little red felt heart.

Next, I sew with neat but not fancy stitches around the edges of the figure, again you can use coloured thread to correspond with your intent.

I leave a gap and then stuff the poppet with some off cuts of felt but also herbs and spices; and I often add a crystal too. You can use all sorts of herbs, woods, plants, roots and spices even salt and rice – go with what suits your intent or what feels right for you. Salt, rice and dried pulses are good if your poppet is larger as they fill up the space nicely and work for purification, protection, negative energy and in the case of rice prosperity too. Charge each item as you add it. Then when your poppet is full sew it up and I like to charge it with my intent again once completed.

I like to set the poppet on my altar and recharge him occasionally with my intent. Some people choose to bury the poppet once it is made, allowing the universe to work the magic, the choice is yours.

Your poppet can be made with just plain stuffing and one special crystal inside. A red felt poppet with a heart shaped rose quartz inside would be perfect for love magic.

Spell pouch/mojo bags:

You could make a spell pouch which contains items that are symbolic to the intent of your spell. This might contain crystals and herbs that support your need, some of your hair to represent you etc. You make the bag whilst visualising your intent coming to fruition. Spell pouches work well because you can add layers of magic by corresponding the colour of the bag with the crystals and the herbs to your intent, each adding another boost of power. Bags can also be fed regularly with magic/sachet powder to keep the magic 'alive'. The powder is literally a blend of herbs and spices or an incense blend that has been ground to a fine powder. I have included an example of a happiness spell pouch in the spells section of this book.

Magic box

Using the same principle as a spell pouch but use a small box. It could be the small cardboard sort you get presents or items through the post in or you could work with a nice wooden one. Charge all the items for your spell and even write your intent on a piece of paper and place them in the box. I think this works particularly well using crystals as you can keep them safe and also cleanse them and the box when you have finished working with it.

Pendulums

A pendulum can be created from any kind of object that has a bit of weight to it, tie it on a ribbon or cord and you have a pendulum. Hag stones (holey stones) are perfect for this as they already come with a hole in the centre through which to tie your cord. Crystals work brilliantly as pendulums, it is just a matter of finding one that resonates with your energy. They won't all work for you, some of them will be incredibly stubborn and won't answer your questions if the crystal clashes with your energy so you may have to look around and test to see what works for you. I have created some excellent pendulums from crystal tumble stones or quartz points by moulding polymer clay around the end of a crystal to create a loop, baking (as per the clay instructions) and then stringing onto a piece of ribbon.

Remember that a pendulum can only answer 'yes' or 'no' questions, it can't give a reading or answer detailed queries. Try to have an open mind when asking it, don't think or wish the answer to be one way, you may influence it. A pendulum also has no concept of time, it doesn't know the difference (or care) between a day, a week or a year. Be specific when you ask it questions!

Hold the chain or string of a pendulum in a way that is comfortable but allows the crystal to swing freely. Don't hold on too tightly. Try holding the tip of the string/chain between your thumb and forefinger, you can also loop the chain/string over the forefinger if it is too long. Make sure your elbow is resting comfortably.

When you first use your pendulum ask it test questions, such as "please show me a yes" and note which way it swings. It may swing side to side or up and down or even clockwise or anticlockwise. Then ask it to "show me a no". And note how it swings. Thank the pendulum after it has responded to each question. Also ask it to "show me a don't know or unsure".

It may take some time to tune into your pendulum and to

get used to how it works for you. It is also worth cleansing your pendulum regularly as it can pick up energy just as any crystal does.

Runes/lithomancy

Crystal tumbled stones are perfect for making your own set of runes. Gather together a pile of them and draw or paint a rune on each one, it could be Futhark/Elder runes or witch runes. You could even create your own set of symbols to use.

Lithomancy is a form of divination that uses stones and crystals for the reading. Gather together your set of stones (tumbled stones again work well for this) and assign a meaning to each one, the meaning may be an association to the magical properties of the stone or involve colour magic. I have included my own suggested divination meanings to each of the crystals listed in this book (in the reference section). But you could assign your own meanings to each crystal, sit quietly with each one and see what meanings come to you.

Scott Cunningham suggests creating a crystal divination set using 21 stones and assigning each one to a card from the major arcana in tarot.

When you have your set ready, ask a question. You can either draw one or two stones out of a bag for your answer or cast them all out onto a flat surface and read where they fall. Casting mats can be designed to help you with the reading. If you are familiar with reading tarot or oracle card decks you could draw out crystals and place them as you would in a card reading; past, present, future or in the Celtic Cross layout.

I have included my own casting mat design, but you can create your own. You could include sections such as; home, love, head, work, relationships, family, finances, business, money, protection, friends, health and emotions.

Once you have 'cast' your stones take the reading depending

on where they fall, this is a guide to assist:

Crystals in the set spaces – relate directly to that area.

Crystals that fell right off the board – not an issue at this time.

Crystals straddling sections – influences are in both areas.

Crystals just off the edge of the board – may come in to play in these areas in the very near future.

Crystals touching each other in the same section – energies are linked and should be read as such.

Crystals towards the centre of the board – these are closely linked with the querent and matter/issue.

Groups of crystals together – that area is very important in the reading.

Crystals touching each other from different sections – the energies of both areas are linked.

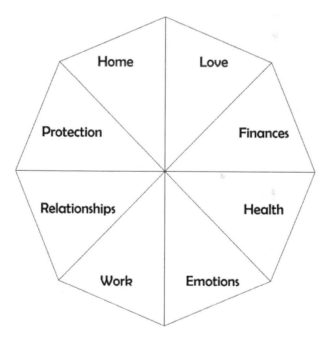

Wands

I don't use a huge array of magical tools, I tend to go with what I have to hand, but I do seem to have collected a few beautiful wands over the years. Crystals lend themselves to being wand tips and decorations, not only adding to the beauty but also the power. Tipping a wand with crystal brings a focal point for the energy to discharge from.

You can purchase some wonderful creative wands, but they are also fairly straightforward to make. Find yourself a suitably sized stick, preferably dropped on the ground by a tree but if you must remove it direct please ask permission from the tree before cutting. And leave an offering. You can leave your stick 'au natural' with the bark still on or you could sand it down and even draw or paint designs and symbols onto it. Then using trusty glue or copper wire fix your crystal to the end or around the handle. You could make wands with specific crystals for particular intents. So, for love magic you might create a wand with a rose quartz tip.

Scrying

Scrying is a form of divination that means looking into a surface and reading the images. It can be done with a dish of water, a puddle, flames, smoke or similar but it also works well with polished crystals. The familiar crystal ball is of course one of the most recognised forms. Crystal balls can be expensive, but you can get them in all sizes and in different qualities/grades of crystal. The purer the crystal the more money you pay but I actually prefer mine to have inclusions, I think it helps create images to read.

Scrying can also be worked with the shiny surface of a crystal, something like a piece of black obsidian works really well. John Dee, a famous metaphysician used a black mirror made from polished obsidian.

Experiment and see what crystal size, colour and shape works best for you. Clear your mind and focus on the surface of the crystal. I find it best to look just across the top of the surface and sort of unfocus my eyes a bit, if that makes sense! Ask your question and see what images, symbols or reflections you see. Then you will need to interpret them...

Crystal water

Water (or any liquid come to that, although water is generally pure and takes on the energy of the crystal well) can be charged with the magical power of a crystal. You can even get special water bottles that have crystal infills. But crystal water or crystal elixir as it is often called, is easy to make yourself. You will need to check that the crystal is SAFE to drop into water, make sure it won't disintegrate and that it isn't toxic, as that would be bad... very bad.

Crystal essence is water that has been imbued with the energy of a single specific crystal. An elixir is usually a mixture of essences blended with an intent in mind.

The most straightforward way to create a crystal essence is to drop a crystal into a glass or bottle of water. Cover with a lid and leave in the sunlight or moonlight for a while, a few hours or overnight will be fine.

The safer method is to put the crystal inside a container before popping that into water. This way you make sure that no toxic elements leak out directly into the water. Place the crystal in a small glass or bottle and then place that into a larger container that has the water in.

Your prepared crystal essence can then be mixed with another made from a different crystal to combine the energy or used on its own.

The water can be drunk, add to the power by stating your intent before you sip the water.

Use to bathe an area of your body or add to bath water.

Anoint your pulse points, chakras, altars or magical tools.

Dab onto candles and pouches for spell work.

Feed your plants with the water.

Sprinkle around your home to clear out negative energy.

Crystal altar

As a witch I have an altar, OK I own up...I have several of them. Each one has a specific purpose, I have a garden altar where I leave offerings to nature and any sun, moon or weather magic spells. Then I have an altar to my matron goddess, The Cailleach and I have a small altar to Ganesha (for any requests to clear blockages and get things moving). Also, a work in progress is my altar to the sun god Belanos, which will include sunstones and goldstones for sure. I also have a working altar indoors where I leave any offerings and spells in progress. Add to that the altar for my spirit animal guide, the wild boar and a very small altar on my desk (items placed on a drink coaster) and I have quite a collection. Any spell workings done with crystals can be placed on an altar of your choosing of course. If it is a spell pouch it could be carried with you, placed beside your bed or under your pillow if you don't have an altar. If you want to work seriously with crystals, then how about a crystal altar? Create a space (indoors or outside) to put your crystal collection upon, crystals for charging and clearing, crystal spell work and any objects that help to connect with the crystals. A dish of water, salt and earth for clearing. Incense and candles for the same purpose and any items that you feel are associated with crystal magic.

Working magic with crystals

Let's assume that you have cleansed and cleared your crystals before you start to work any magic with them. Your stone will also need to have the specific intent sent into it for your spell. Pick a stone that feels right. Generally, you probably wouldn't use a moonstone in a sun spell because it would be a conflict of energy but who knows? Maybe it is the balance of opposites that is needed for the spell to work. TRUST your feelings. Also remember to be clear and specific with any spell work. You need to give the crystal exact and specific instructions about what you need from it. You also need to believe in what you are doing. If your will and intent is not strong (Obi Wan...) then your spell will not have enough power to work properly. A half-hearted or doubted spell will either fail dismally or will go off in a very unexpected direction. Working a spell when you are in a hurry or feeling unwell is also not advisable, the chaotic energy will affect the spell in all the wrong kind of ways.

Crystal healing

Crystals are wonderful to use for healing, they give out huge amounts of healing energy whether you use them directly on a person or use them for distance healing.

At the beginning of a healing session hold the crystal/s in your hand and ask that the divine/angels/deity bless them and ask that the healing be for the highest good. Always remember to give thanks after healing as well.

Use your intuition when you work with crystal healing, be guided by your instinct as to what crystals you need and where the crystal wants you to take it, you may find you want to lay the crystals on the body or that you want to spiral them around a few inches away without contact. You may feel the crystal 'pull' at certain points, be guided by this.

Using a pair of crystals works well for healing – use one to remove pain, negative energies and blockages and use the other to energise and fill the body with positive energy. Always remember to cleanse any crystals used for healing afterwards, you don't want them to carry the negative illness energy with them!

Crystal aura cleansing

You can work with crystals using colour magic; the colours are absorbed through your skin. Psychically your energy field or your aura taken them in and distribute them throughout your body via the chakras.

Because your aura filters out negative energies and emotions it can become discoloured and needs regular cleansing and re-energising.

To cleanse your aura using crystals, find the edge of your aura with your hands (you should feel a pressure/resistance a few inches away from your body). Take two crystals (your choice, go with what you feel is right) one crystal in each hand and spiral the crystals around the body from top to toe at the edge of your aura (usually easier if you have a friend to do this for you). Spiral anti clockwise to remove negative energies and then spiral clockwise to energise your aura.

Crystals and psychic abilities

Crystals are incredibly useful to enhance and amplify our psychic abilities. I keep a quartz crystal in my tarot bag to cleanse the cards; I also lay out three amethyst stones when I do a tarot reading to help amplify the meanings.

At home and at work

Crystals can be used at home and at your place of work to improve the atmosphere and bring harmony. If you have a place where egos clash on a regular basis put out a small bowl of multi coloured crystal chips to help keep the moods stable. Keep a crystal by your computer to soak up any negative energy or keep your favourite crystal close by so that you can hold it when you get stressed. Keep money drawing crystals in your purse.

Carry crystals to help protect you or place them around your home to keep unwanted energies out. Crystals can be used in the work place or at home to keep away gossip, keep your possessions safe, to avoid confrontational calls and to protect you from jealousy and anger. Set dishes of dark and earthy coloured crystals in your home or work place if you are near to electricity pylons or telephone masts to absorb the negative energies they give you. Crystals are also useful to carry for protection and safety whilst travelling.

Crystals and children

Children work beautifully with crystals; they seem to have an instinctive understanding of how they work. If a child is feeling poorly or is worried about something or has nightmares, ask them to select a crystal to keep them safe or to make them feel better.

Crystals and animals

Animals respond incredibly well to crystal healing. Water that has had a crystal sitting in it overnight can be used for healing, vitality and to keep fleas at bay. Crystals can be placed under a pet's bed to keep them calm or good natured. A crystal can be attached to a pet's collar to keep them safe and from straying too far.

Crystals and the environment

Humans have done quite a lot of damage to Mother Earth and we can help in some small way at least to repair some of the damage. Keep a small dish of crystals on a table or your altar specifically for healing the environment, on a regular basis pick up one of the crystals and focus on sending healing to a particular place that you know requires it.

You can also use photographs of places and surround the picture with healing crystals. Burying small pieces of crystal on a damaged site can also help.

Crystal grids

A crystal grid is a geometric pattern of crystals, each one charged with intent and adding its own power to the other crystals in the grid. I think crystal grids are one of the most powerful crystal set ups you can use, they utilise sacred geometry and all sorts of sciencey stuff including tapping into the universal energy and ley lines, but we will stick with how to make them and leave the 'why they work' and just call it magic...

First of all, you need to decide what your intent is for creating the grid. They can be created for just about any purpose. Make sure your intent is clear and specific though because you don't want the 'power' wandering off in unspecified directions.

You can draw out a sacred geometry pattern to work from or print one from the net, but I prefer to work intuitively, whatever way works best for you. A hexagon is a good shape to start with, but you can also use triangles, squares, circles, stars, a spiral or the infinity symbol.

I start with the centre stone, this creates the key point or the power stone, this stone is the amplifier, the connector for the whole grid. I like to use a larger crystal as the centre stone, whilst this isn't absolutely essential it does seem to 'conduct' the power more efficiently.

Don't feel you can't create a crystal grid if you can't afford to buy a big crystal, even if you only have a small selection of tumble stones you can still create an effective grid.

How many surrounding stones you use is up to you and the size of grid you want to create. I also like to charge each stone with the intent as I place it. Start with a basic design and see where your intuition takes you – there is no right or wrong.

To choose the crystals for your grid you can go with your instinct or look up the meanings or even just work with the colour that you feel is right for your intent. You can also add other items into the grid such as business cards, photos or items of jewellery. You can add more than one 'ring' of stones around your centre stone, each new layer will increase and amplify energies. Go with your intuition, what stones you have and the amount of space you have to work with. I recommend you put your grid in a safe place where it won't be disturbed by pets or small children. You may only feel that the grid needs to be left up for an hour or two, you may want to leave it in place for days or weeks – getting everyone to step around a 4' crystal grid in the centre of the living room probably isn't practical...You might like to light candles and incense as you create the grid as well.

Once your grid is all set up you need to activate it. Some people like to use a specific crystal or metal wand to activate each stone in the grid, personally I just use a quartz crystal point, but the choice is yours as to what you use (and what you can afford) a well-aimed finger works as well. Once you are all set up take a moment to calm and centre yourself, then say out loud your intent, it might just be a statement, an affirmation or if you are poetic you could say it in verse.

As you state your intent, point your activation wand/crystal or your finger at the centre stone and visualise energy coming up from the earth (or down from the sky) through your body, down your arm and out through your hand into the centre crystal (you don't need to make actual contact with the crystal) then move your wand from crystal to crystal around the grid linking the energy beam from one stone to the next repeating your intent as you go.

Once you have linked all the stones take an overall look at the grid and visualise your required outcome. Then ground yourself and let the grid do its work. You should instinctively know when the grid is done and when you can dismantle it, or you may feel that it needs longer and requires recharging later, if it needs recharging just repeat the activation sequence again.

Don't ignore your grid, I am not suggesting it will need recharging every day but take some time every few days just to notice it and re-visualise your intent.

If you chose to place other items in your grid they will charge nicely with the energy and in the case of jewellery for instance can be taken out and worn, thereby carrying the energy from the grid with you.

If you have the room you can create a crystal grid large enough for you to sit in, this is wonderful for re-energising yourself. When you do take a crystal grid apart don't forget to cleanse all the crystals you used.

Power wheel

I don't really have a proper name for this type of creation – power wheel, medicine wheel, crystal wheel...you may feel the need to call it something completely different but whatever the name of it this wheel is a powerful source of energy to be directed to whatever intent you feel the need for. It is like a big visual spell based upon a crystal grid.

I like to start with a central feature whether it is a crystal a candle or a card of some sort – it gives the focus of intent. I then fan out in circles (or you could spiral it) using whatever I am drawn to use. If your intent is to bring things towards you (money, love, luck etc.) then place the items in the circle in a deosil (clockwise) way, if you want to get rid of something (bad habits, negativity etc.) then place the items in a pattern widdershins (anti-clockwise).

If your wheel is all about prosperity, success and personal growth you could use oracle cards that all have positive affirmations on, green, yellow and orange candles (for success, happiness and prosperity) and herbs associated with the same intent. For the crystals I would use a lot of green ones such as green aventurine and citrine for success but also add in some quartz to amplify them all. You can add in flower petals, tarot cards, small statues, photographs or anything else that seems to fit.

Be creative and go with what works for you!

I leave the wheel creations in place for as long as feels necessary, sometimes the wind will blow the parts around as I usually create my wheels in the conservatory so during the summer the doors are open.

Once the wind had done its work it usually feels like the right time to dismantle it. Otherwise it gets left alone until I feel the wheel has done the work required.

The cards and crystals get cleansed and put away and if I have used herbs I burn them and scatter the ashes on the garden.

Meditation beads

Your mind can sometimes tend to wander when you are meditating which leads to a loss of concentration. For practising meditation, meditation beads can act as a kind of 'anchor' or grounding point enabling you to focus better. This can be extremely useful especially if you are feeling tired when you meditate.

Then, if your mind is too active and over-energised (darn those mind monkeys), meditation beads will prevent you from becoming distracted or daydreaming. And, because the beads are moved in rhythm with your breathing, it helps you maintain your concentration.

Meditation beads can be used in a number of ways. A popular method is to hang the string between your thumb and your third finger, traditionally in your right hand. Using your middle finger, you rotate the beads one bead at a time towards yourself, each time you repeat the mantra and take a breath.

A variation of this method is to hang the string on your middle finger and rotate the beads one at a time in the same fashion, only this time you use your thumb.

You begin the procedure at the first bead and repeat the process with all of the beads, continuing around the loop until you once again reach the start.

On my meditation beads, each bead signifies a different purpose - as I rotate the bead I say quietly to myself a mantra with that specific intent, for instance when I reach the friends bead I say 'I give thanks for my wonderful friends', when I am on the Cailleach bead I say 'I give blessings and honour the Cailleach for guiding me'.

You can have different beads for different purposes as I have done, or you can have a string of plain beads all the same colour, it is your choice, use whatever works for you.

Mala beads or prayer beads are necklaces created with 108 beads, these are used to keep count during mantras/chants for meditation.

I actually have several, the main set I made myself using a mixture of glass, wood and natural crystal beads. Another set I have is purely for meditating with The Cailleach, so I have used all black and turquoise crystal beads to represent her. You can work with whatever beads you prefer. Real crystal beads can be expensive, but you can get hold of strings of semi-precious beads fairly inexpensively, just be careful which crystals you choose, the more precious the stone, the higher the price. But working with real crystals will add to the feel and the magical energy. If money doesn't allow though...create your own with plastic and wooden beads, it is the intent that matters.

Candle magic

I love to combine crystals with candle magic. Either placing crystals around or in front of the candle or small crystal chips can be set into the candle itself. This gives your magic an extra boost, drawing energy from the crystals. If the wax is warm enough, you can push small crystal chips into the candle. Otherwise dig out a small cavity under the base of the candle and push the crystal in. If you use the beeswax sheet candles you can easily push a small crystal chip into the bottom or the sides. If you make your own candles you can drop small crystals into the wax before it sets.

Elements

Each crystal corresponds to one of the elements, sometimes two. (see the list at the end of this book). But crystals can be used in ritual or spells to represent the four quarters. Choose ones that resonate with you and charge them with the energy of each direction. You can also dab them with a corresponding oil blend or waft them through incense that represents the element. Crystals can also be 'soaked' in a dish of dried herbs to draw up the element energy.

A year of stones

There are specific stones associated with each month of the year and if you choose to use the stone corresponding to your birth month it could provide you with a seriously good connection and an extra oomph to your magical workings. Perhaps wear a piece of jewellery with your birthstone set in, carry a tumble stone with you or place a gemstone on your altar. The list seems to vary depending upon country and time period.

Birthstones

January – garnet
February – amethyst, bloodstone
March – aquamarine, bloodstone, jade (nephrite), jasper
April – diamond, Herkimer diamond, rock crystal
May – agate, carnelian, chrysoprase, emerald
June – alexandrite, carnelian, cat's eye, moonstone, pearl, turquoise
July – carnelian, onyx, ruby, turquoise
August – carnelian, jasper, moonstone, peridot, sardonyx, spinel, topaz
September – chrysolite, lapis lazuli, moonstone, sapphire
October – aquamarine, opal, tourmaline
November – citrine, pearl, topaz
December – bloodstone, lapis lazuli, ruby, tanzanite, turquoise, zircon (blue)

Apparently, the idea of associating stones with the months came from the Bible where a passage in Exodus talks about a beautiful jewel encrusted breastplate featuring twelve stones to represent the sons of Israel and the twelve tribes. But it may have been before then, cultures around the world have used gems and stones as associations and correspondences to birth dates, months and the zodiac.

Which leads us to crystals that correspond with the signs of the zodiac (your sun sign).

Zodiac stones

You can work with a stone associated to your own zodiac sign to bring you a personal connection to your magic. Or you could use a stone that corresponds to the zodiac sign that you are in (astrologically) when you work your magic. Or you could tie in a zodiac crystal to represent the intent that you want to work with, so as an example a Mercury crystal would be good for a communication spell.

Aquarius – amethyst, fluorite, garnet, hematite, labradorite, turquoise

Pisces – amethyst, bloodstone, blue lace agate, fluorite, jade (nephrite), larimar, turquoise

Aries – bloodstone, blue kyanite, citrine, garnet, green aventurine, hematite, jade (nephrite), jasper, red aventurine

Taurus – amber, blue kyanite, carnelian, chrysocolla, chrysoprase, copper, jade/jade (nephrite), malachite, red jasper, rhodonite, rose quartz, sapphire

Gemini – agate, agate (blue lace), agate (moss), celestite, chalcedony, citrine, howlite, jade (nephrite), quartz, serpentine, watermelon tourmaline

Cancer – calcite (orange), carnelian, chrysoprase, citrine, emerald, moonstone, silver

Leo – amber, carnelian, citrine, garnet, gold, labradorite, onyx, pyrite, quartz, rhodochrosite, sunstone, tiger's eye, zircon

Virgo – agate (moss), amethyst, aventurine, carnelian, chrysoberyl, garnet, howlite, jasper, snowflake obsidian, sugilite, watermelon tourmaline

Libra – aventurine, blue kyanite, chrysolite, citrine, jade/jade (nephrite), lepidolite, moonstone, peridot, rose quartz, tourmaline

Scorpio – amethyst, beryl (aquamarine), bloodstone,

citrine, fluorite, jasper, labradorite, malachite, moonstone, rhodochrosite, rose quartz, turquoise, unakite

Sagittarius – amethyst, copper, goldstone, labradorite, lapis lazuli, obsidian (black), smoky quartz, selenite, sodalite, topaz, turquoise

Capricorn – amethyst, fluorite, garnet, hematite, jet, malachite, obsidian, onyx, quartz, smoky quartz, ruby, tiger's eye

Petrified wood covers each of the zodiac signs.

And if you want to narrow it down to crystals to work with on a daily basis, here is a list of some that are associated with days of the week:

Days
Sunday – amber, carnelian, diamond, sunstone, tiger's eye, topaz

Monday – aquamarine, moonstone, pearl, quartz, selenite

Tuesday – bloodstone, emerald, flint, garnet, hematite, rhodonite, ruby

Wednesday – agate, amethyst, citrine, lodestone, mica, pumice

Thursday – amethyst, carnelian, cat's eye, emerald, lepidolite, sapphire, sugilite

Friday – cat's eye, coral, emerald, jade, lapis lazuli, malachite, rose quartz

Saturday – coral, diamond, hematite, jet, obsidian, serpentine, turquoise

It seems we probably have the Sumerians to thank for stones associated with astrology, among other things, as they were very clever people!

Moon phases
If you like to work your spells in tune with the phases of the

moon here are some crystals and their phase correspondences (for more details on working with the moon phases, see my book Pagan Portals: Moon Magic):

Full moon – moonstone, sunstone, smoky quartz, selenite

Waxing moon – carnelian, tiger's eye, rose quartz, labradorite, citrine

Waning moon – citrine, quartz, bloodstone, obsidian

What happens if a crystal breaks?

It doesn't happen very often thankfully, but it is heart-breaking and perhaps a little worrying when it does. But don't panic! It isn't a message from the gods warning that you will be struck down, seriously it isn't. Basically, it is a natural item and if it gets too hot, too cold, too wet or dropped on a hard floor it will break, hey stuff happens. Actually, I had a crystal develop a crack right across it recently, it was the crystal I use on top of my monthly new moon abundance spell. Now it could mean that I have been spending too much money (and it would be absolutely right) or it is more likely the result of me dropping it accidentally from a great height onto a solid slate floor. The said crystal is now sitting outside in the garden, cracked but still pretty. I felt it had done the work it needed too, so I thanked it and was drawn to place it outside. It now sits helping the plants to grow.

Some say that when a crystal cracks or breaks the magic is done and whatever you were working with is now complete. But only you can decide if that feels right to you or not.

Your broken or cracked crystal will still hold the same magical properties that it did before. In fact, if it splits into two or more pieces then you are in luck, because you have just ended up with more crystals, smaller pieces but still more in quantity.

You may feel that a broken crystal needs to be re-purposed (as I did with mine and popped it in the garden) or you might get the inkling that it has finished working for you and needs to be passed on to someone else. Trust your intuition.

Remember that crystals absorb energy, water and light. Look after them, cleanse them regularly and try not to drop them on the floor...

Touchstone

You can keep a touchstone just for you. A unique personal power source of energy that is aligned with your own vibes. Pick a stone that resonates with you, it might correspond with your zodiac sign perhaps or just be a crystal that you love. Cleanse and charge it in the full moon, then keep it by your bed for seven nights. This will create a powerful stone for you to draw personal energy from, one that is connected to you directly. Recharge it regularly under the full moon.

A crystal discovery meditation

Make yourself comfortable in a place where you won't be disturbed.

Close your eyes and focus on your breathing...deep breaths in...deep breaths out.

As your world around you dissipates you find yourself standing at the mouth of a cave, the entrance is quite large, and you feel comfortable walking forward towards it.

The air is cool and still, but you feel warm and pleasant.

As you walk, you realise the cave goes back quite a way, so you keep taking steps forward.

You put your hands out on either side of you to feel the cave walls, they are cool to the touch.

Once you have walked a short distance the cave suddenly opens out.

A huge space is now in front of you with a ceiling that reaches high up so far you cannot see the top.

There are flame torches around the walls lighting up the whole floor before you.

Everything glitters and sparkles...

There are large rock formations scattered across the ground, each one a different colour, and each one shining and twinkling in the light from the torches.

Looking around the walls you realise those too are all covered in shimmering crystals of all colours and types.

The view is breath taking.

You make your way to a large flat rock in the centre of the cavern and sit down.

Take in the view, look left and right and all around you.

What colours and shapes there are, such a variety it is quite overwhelming.

You sit quietly just taking it all in and feeling the vibrating energy coming from all of the crystals, it isn't too much, it just makes you feel happy and content.

There is a sudden noise to one side of you and something small bounces and pings across the floor, coming to rest at your feet.

You bend down and pick up a small crystal…what colour is it? Do you recognise the type? A name comes into your mind.

This is your sacred stone, one that you need to work with to help you at this moment in time.

You hold the stone in the palm of your hand and wait for any messages…

Once you are ready you pop the stone in your pocket.

Take a last look around you and the wonderous view.

Know that you can always come back here for guidance.

Slowly make your way back out from the cavern, through the entrance and outside.

Gently come back to this reality, wriggling your fingers and toes.

Remember to ground.

CRYSTAL SPELLS

This section will hopefully give you some basic spell outlines and suggestions as well as some specific spells to work with. As always trust your intuition and go with what works for you. Some of them are 'multi-purpose' and can be tweaked and used as a template to work any kind of intent with such as the candle magic and spell pouch spells. Focus on your intent and pick the crystals and ingredients that you feel will help direct the spell to your desired outcome.

Keep it with you
Ultimately the simplest crystal spell is to charge a tumble stone with your intent and carry it with you – straightforward and fuss free. Alternatively place a tumble stone under your pillow or beside your bed to absorb the energy and magic.

Petition spell
Write out your desire or wish on a slip of paper, fold it up neatly and place a corresponding crystal on top of it. Keep it on your altar or somewhere you can see it regularly.

Releasing spell
Hold a crystal of your choice in your hand whilst you stand outside in the rain, under the shower or in the bath. Then allow the energy of the crystal to wash away your worries or anxiety. Howlite, moss agate and calcite are particularly good for this.

Direction
Use a crystal point when casting a circle or directing energy to a spell to focus that energy and increase the power.

Happiness candle spell

Gather together ingredients that shout 'happiness' to you, using whatever you have to hand, in your garden or your cupboards. My choice for happiness is citrine but use what you prefer or have to hand. I like to work with candle magic, but tailor the spell to what works for you.

This can be used as a template for any kind of intent. Choose what you want to work towards, it might be prosperity, protection or peace and tailor the crystals and herbs added in to correspond to your spell.

I used:

A yellow candle

A piece of paper with the word 'happiness' written on it

Plants and herbs corresponding to happiness – I used:

Dried marigolds

Dried lavender

Carnelian

Goldstone

Amber

A yellow flower from the garden

A chocolate muffin

A mannaz rune

And of course, a piece of citrine

Place the citrine in the centre and your paper with the word 'happiness' on a safe, fire proof surface. Add your candle and then surround it will any herbs, crystals or other items you feel are needed to add power to the spell.

Charge each item with the intent of happiness as you place them.

When you are ready, sit quietly and visualise your world filled with happiness.

Light the candle and say:

With this candle, happiness I invite in
Joy and laughter to begin
Surround myself and those I love
With much happiness from above

Sit and watch the candle flame and keep the visualisation going until you feel ready to finish. If you use a small candle you can let it burn right out, but please never leave it unattended. If you use a larger candle snuff out the flame and dispose of the candle safely. Return your dried herbs, plants and natural items to the earth or compost bin. Carry the citrine with you or place it on your altar to keep the happiness energy flowing. Cleanse the other crystals and keep them for future use. Eat the cake!

Happiness Charm Bag

A charm or medicine bag can be created with any intent and carried with you or left on your altar. It can also be 're-charged' with energy when you feel the need. Go with your intuition about what to put into your bag. I would suggest dry ingredients because fresh plants and flowers (or cake) will go mouldy and that would make for a pretty icky charm bag. This is a template that can be worked for any intent, choose your crystals and ingredients to correspond with your spell goal.

My suggestion:

Choose a small bag or piece of fabric and ribbon in a colour that says 'happiness' to you (I would use yellow). Add in your items, charging each one with happiness as you go
    I used:
    3 small pieces of citrine
    A piece of goldstone
    Dried rose petals (yellow)
    Dried marigolds

Dried lavender

You can say a chant or just speak your desire whilst creating the bag.

Protection spell

You will need:

A quartz

A crystal to represent fire

A crystal to represent water

A crystal to represent air

A crystal to represent earth

A dish of water

My suggestion: I used a carnelian for fire, a blue lace agate for water, a brown jasper for air and a moss agate for earth.

Place the bowl of water in front of you.

Pick up the earth stone and ask that the element of earth bring stability and steadfastness for protection, pop the crystal in the bowl of water.

Pick up the air stone and ask that the element of air blow away all the negative energy. Pop the crystal in the bowl of water.

Pick up the fire stone and ask that the element of fire bring energy for protection. Pop the crystal in the bowl of water.

Pick up the water stone and ask the element of water to wash away gossip, lies and unkind words aimed towards you. Pop the crystal in the bowl of water.

Then take the clear quartz stone in both hands and see it as a shield around you. Pop the quartz into the bowl of water and visualise it drawing up all the positive energy and strength from the four element crystals. When you feel it is ready take the stones out and tip the water on to the earth.

Dry and cleanse the coloured stones and keep for future use. Dry the quartz and carry it with you for protection.

Creating a talisman or amulet

Talisman - a magically charged object that attracts a desired energy. Talismans bring power and energy to the wearer. Amulet – a magically charged object which deflects unwanted energy and brings protection.

You will need:

A white candle (or colour of your choice)

A quartz or similar boosting/amplifying crystal (if you have one)

A crystal to use as your amulet or talisman

Place the boosting crystal (if using) in front of the candle and light the candle wick.

Hold your talisman/amulet crystal in your hands and visualise your intent/goal/desire and send that energy into the crystal.

When ready place your talisman/amulet crystal so that it touches the base of the booster crystal or the base of the candle.

Leave the crystal there until the candle has burnt out, or for at least an hour (do not leave lit candles unattended).

Then your talisman or amulet is good to go.

You can layer this spell by burning a corresponding incense or passing the talisman/amulet through the smoke. You can also dress the candle in a matching oil blend and/or sprinkle with dried herbs. Or carve symbols into the candle.

Balance spell

We all need a little bit of balance in life on occasion, sometimes more than others.

You will need:

A black candle (or a dark colour)

A white candle (or a light colour)

A clear quartz or a light crystal

An obsidian or dark crystal

Pouch or piece of fabric

Light both candles and place the clear quartz in front of the white candle and the obsidian in front of the black candle. Ask out loud for balance in your life, personal, friendships, relationships, work, home, wherever you need it.

Sit quietly and watch the candle flames for a while. Take note of any messages or images that come to you.

Then pick up both the crystals and swap them over, so the quartz is in front of the black candle and the obsidian is in front of the white candle.

Sit quietly again. Allow the candles to burn out.

Put the crystals in a small pouch or wrap in fabric and carry with you or pop on your altar.

Bath time magic

You will need:

A bath…obviously

Sea salt/Epsom salts/herbs/flower petals/or just good ole bubble bath

Tealights

Several crystal tumble stones

Run the bath and pop in your bath salts and/or herbal mix if using.

Place the crystals around the edge of the bath interspersed with the tea lights (don't put a candle by your head).

Light the tealights.

Carefully sink into the water.

Ask for guidance, messages or just specific energy from the crystals.

Stay in the water and relax until you are ready to come out.

You may have received messages, or you might get them later whilst you are sleeping.

This can be tailored to all kinds of intents. Use coloured candles, herbs that correspond and crystals for your intent. For instance, rose quartz to bring love paired with rose petals is perfect or green aventurine and mint to answer money worries also works well.

Positive energy spell

You will need:

A yellow or pink candle

Several yellow or pink crystals such as citrine or rose quartz

Set the candle in a safe place and arrange the crystals in a circle around it.

Light the candle and sit quietly visualising positive, happy energy filling the crystals.

Allow the candle to burn out, then place each crystal around your home to bring in all the good stuff.

This spell also adapts to bring blessings to a new home.

You can add extra oomph by sitting the crystals in dried herbs and/or dabbing them with an essential oil whilst they charge with the candle.

The crystals can be cleansed and recharged when you feel they need to be.

Money spell

You will need:

A green crystal (I like to use aventurine or malachite)

Slip of paper

Pen

Green, gold or orange candle

Place the crystal in front of the candle and light the candle wick.

Write what you need on the paper, it might be a specific amount of money or just enough money to cover a particular bill, but don't sell yourself short.

Fold the paper three times then pop it under the crystal.

Thank the universe / deity / angels / divine / the force, for providing for you.

Let the candle burn out then bury the stone and paper in the ground. In the garden is perfect but a pot of soil will do.

Once the money arrives dig up the crystal and be thankful.

Letting go spell

This is a spell to banish or release something, it might be an emotion such as fear, or it could be a bad habit or pattern that needs breaking.

You will need:

A crystal of your choice, one you can part with (I like to use smoky quartz or jasper)

Paper and pen

Black or dark candle

Cauldron or fire proof dish.

Light the candle and place the crystal in front of it.

Write that which you wish to be rid of on a slip of paper.

Place the stone on the paper and sit quietly watching the flame and visualise releasing and letting it all go, being rid of it completely. Also remember to visualise filling the void with good, positive energy too.

Then take the stone in one hand and the paper in the other. Light the paper from the candle and allow it to burn out in a safe dish/cauldron.

Then either bury the stone in the earth (away from your property) or throw it in to running water (the ocean or a river).

Walk away without looking back.

Rainbow spell for YOU

This spell is all about you and your own power.

You will need:

Seven crystals, one for each colour of the rainbow; red, orange, yellow, green, blue, indigo (lilac/purple), violet (or clear).

Seven candles, one for each colour of the rainbow, or plain white (optional)

A white cloth if you have one

Place the cloth if you are using one, in front of you. Add the crystals, placing them in a rainbow arch shape.

Add in matching candles if you want or plain white ones, one behind each crystal and light the wicks.

Give them each a different quality that you would like to manifest. Charge each one in your hand and state the intent out loud, so it might be:

Red – courage, passion, energy

Orange – success, personal power

Yellow – happiness, friendship

Green – prosperity, hope

Blue – good health, healing, communication

Indigo – spirituality, faith

Violet – inner sight, clarity

Placing each one back in position when you have charged it with your intent.

When all seven are charged, sit quietly watching the candle flames and wait for any guidance or messages.

Then take each crystal, one by one, blowing out each candle in turn and place the crystals in a pouch to keep with you or in a dish to keep on your altar.

Tap into the energy when you need it by holding the crystal in your hand.

Recharge with the candles again at regular intervals, each full moon works nicely.

Looking for answers

Choose a crystal, be guided by your intuition (but labradorite and moonstone both work well for this) and lie down in a quiet place. Place the crystal on your forehead/third eye and ask your question. Lie still and listen. Make a note of any images or words that come to you. If the answer doesn't come, try writing your question on a piece of paper and place it under the crystal on your altar instead. Look out for signs as you go about your day. Jot down any images or words that come to you, it might not make sense at first but when you come back to it hopefully it will shed some light for you.

Connection

To connect with the divine/deity/higher realms choose a crystal (selenite and quartz work well here) and light some incense. Place the crystal in front of the incense.

Look at the stone, clear your mind and focus on the crystal and allow it to open a connection for you. Listen...

New job spell

Choose a stone that represents success to you, I would go for goldstone or malachite.

Write down your dream job on a slip of paper or take a sheet from the job section of the newspaper and fold it up. Place the crystal on top and leave it out where you will see it.

Recharge the crystal with your intent each day until you get a job.

Give thanks when success is achieved.

Luck spell

Choose 3, 6, 7 or 9 small crystals that represent luck to you. I like to use green aventurine, goldstone or tiger's eye.

Lay them out on a full moon for the night. The next day charge them with the intent of luck and success then pop them in a pouch and carry with you.

Money bag

You will need:

A green pouch

A silver coin

A green crystal, I like to use malachite or green aventurine

Herbs such as basil and mint

Charge your items on a waxing moon (to bring things to you) and carry with you or pop on your altar. The bag and contents can be recharged and 'fed' with more herbs to boost the energy.

A crystal wish dish

Place a dish containing sand or small seeds on a table in your home. Add in a handful of mixed tumble stones. When you feel the need, pick up one of the crystals and make a wish, then make a pattern with the crystals inside the dish with your wish stone at the centre.

The crystals will need to be cleansed every so often.

A note about gratitude...

When we work spells we are asking the universe (or whatever otherworldly being/s you work with) to provide for us, so it makes sense and is only good manners to say thank you. When working with crystals I like to cleanse them when the spell is done and just give a word of thanks. On a bigger scale I like to leave offerings to deity and do something for nature such as feeding the birds. You cannot keep asking for things without giving anything in return...

REFERENCE SECTION

In this part of the book I have made recommendations for certain crystals and magical intentions and what intent to use them for. I have stuck with the more common/readily available stones, there are some amazingly expensive rarer stones, but you will need bottomless pockets for those. Magic can be made from a simple pebble, so I don't see the point in breaking the bank to work with crystals. You don't have to go with my ideas, connect with each of your own crystals and stones and see how they speak to you. Or take spell ideas given by others and tailor and tweak them to suit you, make them personal. As with all crystals I encourage you to connect with each one and find out what it means to YOU. Trust your intuition. This will give you some idea to get started.

Agate

These beauties come in all sorts of shapes and patterns. Agate is part of the chalcedony family. Each one is individual and can have crazy patterns. The agate is formed by minerals filling a hole in a rock. I love meditating and working divination with these as there are so many images to be found in the surface. It is the banding that makes them agate, setting them apart from other forms of chalcedony. Often worn throughout history as a talisman or amulet it was believed to bring good luck and healing. It was also thought to protect against storms and good for children to protect them from danger. Although most agate is natural in colour you can find them dyed in bright colours such as pink, green or blue. A rough agate will usually seem dull and uninteresting until it is sliced and polished. It is believed that a Greek philosopher Theophrastus discovered the stone in the 3rd/4th century BC. He named the stone after the river in which it was found, the Achates, in Italy. (The river is now known as the Dirillo).

Agate magical properties

Perception, wisdom, balance, spirituality, goodwill, peace, memory, concentration, stamina, truth, clarity, honesty, courage, protection, calming, sleep, dreams, strength, longevity, nature, love, anti-stress, energy

The above covers all agate in general but mostly the banded, brown and black (see separate sections for blue lace and moss agate.

Energy:	Projective
Element:	Fire
Planet:	Mercury
Zodiac:	Gemini

Carry moss agate to calm your nerves.
Wear or carry agate to bring you confidence.

Suggested cleansing:

As the original agate stone was found in a river, water is the perfect medium for cleansing.

Agate divination meaning:

Batten down the hatches, a storm is a'comin...Agate can be a sign of a storm or disruption on the horizon. But fore warned is fore armed as they say. Be prepared and take a step back, see both sides of any disagreement and view the situation with clarity and a sensible head. A lot of arguments are storms in a tea cup, don't rise to it and you will weather through it.

Agate (blue lace)

A very pretty pale blue agate stone with white bands and lines.

Blue lace agate is most definitely a stone of communication. It has a very long history of use dating back through many civilisations.

Agate (Blue lace) magical properties

Mediation, spirituality, uplifting, calming, peace, communication, emotions, support, optimism, happiness, protection, cleansing, healing, prosperity, longevity, strength, courage, clarity, success, patience, truth, stress, relaxation, creativity, justice, travel, renewal, understanding, soothing, trust

Energy:	Receptive
Element:	Water
Planet:	Mercury
Zodiac:	Gemini

Place blue lace agate in the east of your home to bring in good health, the south east for abundance and the south west for luck and love, heck just put a bit in every corner!

Suggested cleansing

Rinse in water and dry with a soft cloth or use visualisation or incense smoke. Charge under the moonlight.

Agate (blue lace) divination meaning

Express yourself! Blue lace agate is all about the communication, get talking, voice your opinion, speak your truth. Open your mouth and shout about it!

Agate (Moss)

A green and white version of agate, some of these stones look like they have moss growing over them. Often seen as a stone of gardeners and those that work with the land. It has also been used by warriors, carried with them for strength and victory.

Agate (moss) magical properties

Nature, happiness, prosperity, wealth, longevity, friendship, success, abundance, healing, renewal, fertility, creativity, confidence, strength, love, beginnings, self-esteem, communication, emotions, stress, releasing, hope, trust, depression, growth, finances, cleansing, support, peace, stability, fears, luck, divination

Energy:	Receptive
Element:	Earth
Planet:	Moon
Zodiac:	Virgo, Gemini

Suggested cleansing

Cleansing of moss agate works well when placed in amongst nature or the soil, this also charges the stone.

Agate (moss) divination meaning

Moss agate is a stone of growth and this could mean in any area of your life, where does it need growth? Money, abundance, friends, family, love – any number of things could be coming your way, count your blessings.

Amber

A stone of liquid sunshine...although not technically a stone at all, it is the fossilised resin of a coniferous tree (now sadly extinct). It is however incredibly ancient and was apparently one of the first gems to be worn as bling. Jewellery using amber has been found as far back as 8000BCE. The Greek word 'electron' translates as 'amber' which in turn is said to have also been the base for the word 'electricity'. Amber can apparently hold an electrical charge, when rubbed it will produce a negative electrical energy. It has long been a stone of manifestation and luck and one to bring happiness and positive energy. Most amber comes in yellow to orange, but you can often find green amber and even red, blue and black on occasion. It is nearly always transparent and can sometimes include a small insect or piece of plant that became trapped in the sticky resin before it hardened. Cloudy amber is caused by air being trapped when the resin was soft. Amber always feels warm to the touch, which led to the belief that it possessed a life. It has also been associated with Akash or the fifth element, spirit, that which binds together the four elements of earth, air, fire and water. You can also find amberoid which is several small pieces of amber which have been fused together with heat and oil.

Amber magical properties:

Manifesting, energy, beauty, sun magic, power, wishes, intellect, clarity, wisdom, balance, purification, protection, psychic abilities, healing, calm, patience, love, sensuality, good luck, marriage, abundance, success, vitality, joy, sexuality, cleansing, stress, harmony, creativity

Energy:	Projective
Element:	Fire, Spirit
Planet:	Sun
Zodiac:	Leo

Place a piece of amber on your altar to add oomph to all your magical workings.

Keep with you to protect against curses and hexes.

Amber is very grounding, don't wear it all the time.

Suggested cleansing

Amber can become cloudy when it has absorbed negative energy. Cleanse with warm water. Don't leave in direct sunlight as it can become brittle. Amber can easily be scratched and will be damaged by chemicals and cleaning solutions. Don't put it near a flame, it can burn.

Amber divination meaning:

Get manifesting! Amber brings you opportunities galore. Time to put your hopes, wishes and desires out into the universe because this stone says "yes, you can have it all". It brings hot fiery sunshiny energy to bring all the goodies your way.

Amethyst

Possibly one of the most well-known crystals and one that is worked with a lot. The name amethyst comes from the Greek word 'amethystos' which translates as 'non-intoxicating'. Ancient Romans and Greeks believed it would prevent them from getting drunk...wonder how well that worked for them? Amethyst is mentioned in the Egyptian Book of the Dead; a heart shaped piece being placed on the deceased body to help them travel peacefully to the next otherworld. Amethyst is also a favourite of Buddha. Amethyst is crystalline quartz, the colour ranging from lilac to dark purple which is created by iron impurities and sometimes exposure to natural radiation. Once naturally heated parts of it will turn yellow, becoming citrine – the mixed stone then becoming ametrine. There are also some ametrine that have been artificially heated to create a similar result. It is widely considered to be a soothing and spiritual stone but also one of change and transition. Amethyst holds transitional energy and can help bring about changes within your life in a smooth and calm way.

Amethyst magical properties

Peace, protection, success, good luck, hidden knowledge, legal issues, spirituality, contentment, soothing, relaxation, calm, hope, patience, transformation, changes, breaking patterns, grounding, guilt, overcoming addictions, business matters, judgement, clarity, courage, travel, psychic protection, sleep, anxiety, focus, understanding, happiness, justice, intuition, inspiration, channelling, meditation

Exchange pieces of amethyst with your loved one to enhance your love bonds (heart shaped pieces would be perfect for this).

Pop a piece of amethyst in with your tarot, oracle cards or runes to help with your intuition.

Amethyst is an excellent all-round healing stone.

Keep amethyst with you to help you focus and aid your memory.

Energy:	Receptive
Element:	Water
Planet:	Jupiter, Neptune
Zodiac:	Pisces, Scorpio, Sagittarius
Birthstone:	February

Suggested cleansing

Amethyst clusters can be used to place other stones upon to cleanse them.

Cleanse amethyst under the moonlight. Don't place in the sunlight, it will fade.

Amethyst divination meaning

A beautiful butterfly must first begin as a caterpillar and go through a transition to become what it is meant to be. Transition and changes can sometimes be difficult and hard work, but it is always worth the effort. Don't fight against the changes, go with the flow and know that change is inevitable but worthwhile in the end.

Aventurine (green)

Green aventurine is the most commonly found, although it comes in other colours such as orange, blue and brown. It is a variety of quartz that contains small flakes that sparkle, these are usually muscovite mica but will sometimes be hematite or goethite.

Aventurine magical properties

Balance, decisions, motivation, leadership, dreams, visualisation, creativity, luck, money, anxiety, calm, opportunities, happiness, adventure, love, courage, truth, comfort, support, healing, peace, connection, perception, intellect, psychic abilities

Energy:	Projective
Element:	Air
Planet:	Mercury, Mars
Zodiac:	Aries

Pop a piece of aventurine in your purse to attract money to you.

Aventurine can help open your third eye and aid with perception.

A really good general all round wellbeing stone.

Suggested cleansing

Cleanse under running water. Recharge in the sunlight preferably near green plant life.

Aventurine divination meaning

Whoohoo! This is your lucky day. This stone brings luck and opportunities in abundance. Keep an eye out for doors opening and all the good things happening. The luck of the Gods is with you...don't waste your chance!

Bloodstone

This gem has such a brilliant name, conjures up images of Vikings for me...Bloodstone is a dark green variety of chalcedony/quartz that is speckled with red or brown spots (which are splodges of iron oxide). The red/brown spots looking a little like blood, hence the name. How many or how few spots you get depends on each gemstone. During medieval times it was believed that the stone was created when Christ's blood fell and stained the jasper stone at the bottom of the cross during his crucifixion. Symbols were then carved into the stones to depict the crucifixion, leading to the stone being nick named 'martyr's stone'. Bloodstone is sometimes referred to as heliotrope which is made from two Greek words 'helios' and 'tropos' which translates as 'sun to turn'. Bloodstone has been used magically for several thousands of years, primarily to help gain control of negative spirits it was also worn to prevent the wearer being cheated or deceived.

Bloodstone magical properties:

Organisation, adaptability, anxiety, clarity, concentration, renewal, energy, self-confidence, connection, calm, protection, breaking barriers, selfishness, mysticism, insight, spirituality, truth, intuition, creativity, guidance, strength, healing, victory, wealth, money, power, invisibility, deception, negative energy, divine connection, past life, dreams

Energy:	Projective
Element:	Fire, Earth
Planet:	Mars
Zodiac:	Aries, Pisces, Scorpio
Birthstone:	February, March

Use bloodstone with your spell work to increase the power of the working.

Bloodstone will increase your consciousness.

Suggested cleansing

Cleanse and recharge under running water or in sunlight.

Calcite (orange)

I have a large piece of orange calcite…it looks like a slab of raw salmon…Calcite is made of calcium carbonate and is found in many geological environments as a part of sedimentary rocks, limestone being one. Calcite is from the Greek word 'chalix' which translates as 'lime'. You will also find calcite in the form of stalactites and stalagmites in caves.

Calcite (orange) magical properties

Amplification, energy, protection, grounding, centring, purification, peace, calm, emotions, balance, fear, depression, problems, power, potential, breaking patterns, changes, inspiration, creativity, positive energy, wealth, abundance, leadership, perseverance, finances, confidence, determination, money, opportunities, clarity, productivity, release

Energy:	Receptive
Element:	Earth
Planet:	Sun
Zodiac:	Cancer

Calcite causes the optical trick of 'double refraction', when you place calcite over an image it can cause it to appear double. This gives the stone the ability to double up the power when working any spell. Wear or place on your altar during the spell working.

Calcite will help aid your memory and bring clarity to decisions.

An excellent stone to meditate with it opens doorways to your spirituality.

Suggested cleansing

Cleanse under running water, charge with other quartz crystals.

Carnelian

Another from the chalcedony family this comes in shades of red, orange, pink and brown, the colour is caused by iron oxide. Two schools of thought about the name, it may come from the Latin word 'cornum' which means 'cherry' (and some of them do look like cherries to be fair) or that it derives from the Latin word 'carneus' which means 'flesh'. The Egyptian Book of the Dead tells that carnelians were placed in tombs for protection in the life after. They would also carry it with them in the living world to provide a source of energy. Carnelian was often used in seal rings to stamp into letter wax.

Carnelian magical properties

Grounding, protection, calm, concentration, confidence, self-worth, success, courage, creativity, negative energy, direction, control, organisation, opportunity, planning, psychic protection, jealousy, hate, harmony, depression, doubt, patience, stability, vitality, motivation, stamina, passion, truth, love, faith, honesty, trust, luck, abundance

Energy:	Projective
Element:	Fire
Planet:	Sun
Zodiac:	Taurus, Leo
Birthstone:	May, June, July, August

Carnelian spell work

Place carnelian in your home to bring peace and harmony.

Put carnelian in the west of your home for creativity and in the south for luck and success.

Carnelian will bring the 'va va' back into your 'voom' and give you a new love of life.

Wear carnelian to bring you clarity and courage.

Suggested cleansing

Cleanse under warm running water and recharge in the sunlight. Keep a carnelian in with other stones to help cleanse them.

Celestite

A very angelic crystal with its name coming from Latin, meaning 'heavenly or celestial'. It is indeed a very pretty pale blue colour. Found where sandstone and limestone have begun to break down the crystals grow in thin, nodular forms and is often found growing within a geode. Often used to work directly with your guardian angel and a divine connection.

Celestite magical properties

Divine, spirit work, love, clarity, decisions, meditation, communication, peace, dreams, stress, healing, astral travel, calming, uplifting, harmony, happiness, spirituality

Energy:	Receptive
Element:	Air, Water
Planet:	Neptune, Venus
Zodiac:	Gemini

Celestite is an excellent stone to bring about balance in your life.

Keep celestite with you when writing or speaking to increase confidence and flow of creativity.

Celestite is also believed to be a listening stone that will provide guidance when needed.

Suggested cleansing

Cleanse next to hematite or under the starry sky. This stone can be charged by the sun or the moon dependent upon what type of energy you want to fill it with.

Celestite divination meaning

It brings the heavenly, celestial power to your doorstep. You may want to look outside the mundane and search for a more divine answer to your situation. Tap into the connections outside of the world wide web to find guidance.

Chrysocolla

Apparently, this is a very wise and clever stone...the ancient Egyptians called it the 'wise stone of conciliation'. It grows in clusters or a crust and is often found intertwined with other types of crystal. Chrysocolla is a blue/green stone made of a unique copper ore. It is a very feminine stone full of energy connected with the sea, water and the divine feminine.

Chrysocolla magical properties

Wisdom, peace, patience, love, soothing, intuition, energy, calming, emotions, fear, strength, clarity, balance, negative energy, insight, releasing, spirituality, psychic abilities, guilt, divine, harmony, communication, meditation

Energy:	Receptive
Element:	Water
Planet:	Venus
Zodiac:	Taurus

A stone of Mother Earth and also carries lunar energy.

Chrysocolla is a really good stone to bring in personal protection.

Suggested cleansing

Cleanse under warm running water, charge next to hematite.

Chrysocolla divination meaning

This packs a punch of strong feminine energy bringing all those watery emotions with it. Tap into your feminine side, allow those emotions to flow. Let it all go baby...Whilst the watery emotions are strong so is the feminine warrior energy. Release the salty tears...dry your eyes and buckle on your sword, don't mess with the feminine!

Chrysoprase

A very pretty, striking green variety of chalcedony which gains its colour from nickel. It is a cryptocrystalline, made from tiny weeny fine crystals. Keep this one out of the sunlight as it can fade quite easily. The name comes from the Greek words 'chrysos' and 'prason' which translate as 'gold' and 'bloom or leek'. The gold part comes from the gold colourings found on the stone.

Chrysoprase magical properties

Courage, strength, wisdom, releasing, selfishness, imagination, happiness, success, balance, break barriers, protection, truth, healing, luck, prosperity, marriage, negative energy, transformation, love

Energy:	Receptive
Element:	Earth
Planet:	Venus
Zodiac:	Taurus, Cancer

Wear or carry with you to bring prosperity, luck and attract money to you.

Chrysoprase really stores energy exceptionally well.

Pop a piece under your pillow to help with relaxation and a good night's sleep.

Suggested cleansing

Cleanse under running water regularly (rain showers are perfect for this stone), charge with quartz crystals.

Chrysoprase divination meaning

Watch out for the 'green eyed monster', this crystal warns of all the bad vibes that bring greed and selfishness. Are you the culprit? Or is someone else directing those energies towards you? Either way, be watchful of it.

Citrine

Citrine is a form of quartz. Natural citrine is fairly uncommon, most of the citrine you find in the shops is created by heat treating amethyst or smoky quartz. It only takes a low temperature to turn the colour to a yellow. The higher the temperature the darker yellow the quartz becomes.

Brazil is the largest citrine source, but they may also come from Argentina, Madagascar, Zaire, Namibia, Spain or Russia. The name may be derived from the French word for lemon which is 'citron'. Although not one of the major stones in ancient cultures, citrine has been mentioned throughout history for over 6000 years. It was used a great deal throughout the first and second century in Greece and Rome, mainly for a talisman against evil, scandal, treachery and overindulging.

Citrine magical properties:

Happiness, joy, sun magic, negative energy, optimism, abundance, depression, stress, success, wealth, healing, intuition, creativity, confidence, changes, self-esteem, protection, psychic powers, fears, clarity, stamina, nightmares

Energy:	Projective
Element:	Fire
Planet:	Sun, Jupiter
Zodiac:	Scorpio
Birthstone:	November

Suggested Cleansing:

Citrine is one of the few stones that never requires cleansing or clearing, it does that itself.

Citrine divination meaning

Happy, happy, happy, happy talk...talk about things you like to do! (Bet you are singing now...). This stone is all about the sunshiny good stuff. It brings joy, luck, happiness and all the fabulous vibes that you can imagine with it. Put a big smile on your face because citrine says 'life is wonderful, make the most of it'!

Fluorite

A very pretty stone made up of calcium fluoride that can be found in many colours, such as purple, blue, white and green and often shades of different colours in one stone. Fluorite was originally called fluorspar. Folklore suggests that this stone houses rainbows. The name comes from the Latin word 'fluo' which translates as 'flow'. It is an excellent stone to absorb negative energy from your environment and also a perfect stone to help amplify your own spiritual connections and sub conscious. It also helps amplify the energy of other stones.

Fluorite magical properties

Magic, imagination, discernment, aptitude, psychic protection, protection, purification, calming, relaxation, tension, anxiety, organisation, structure, challenges, declutter, releasing, support, breaking patterns, intuition, confidence, reassurance, comforting, communication, balance, spirituality, decisions, manifestation, peace, meditation, grounding, healing, cleansing, channelling, past life work, fairy realm, amplifying, memory, power, emotions, depression, stability

Energy: Projective

Element:	Water, Air
Planet:	Neptune
Zodiac:	Scorpio, Aquarius, Pisces

Use with other crystals in spells to open up the channels and allow the energy from other crystals to 'do their thing'.

An excellent stone to work with to help meditate and focus your concentration.

Fluorite will really increase the ooh la la in your life...you have been warned.

Suggested cleansing

Because of its ability to so easily absorb negative energy, cleanse fluorite regularly. Pop under running water to cleanse and charge in sunlight.

Fluorite divination meaning

Connections...fluorite helps make the link between our mind and the divine. In doing so it helps us to tap into our intuition and make connections between what we see and think and what we should actually be doing about it. It builds bridges and pathways for us to follow, allow fluorite to work its magic and show you the way.

Garnet

Carried by warriors for thousands of years the garnet has long been believed to bring protection against injury and even death. A stone of victory but also one that sweeps in with peace and healing. Garnet comes with its own built in anti-theft device, if given to you as a gift or purchased it will grant you the good stuff in life, but if you steal it then be prepared to suffer the consequences. Garnet is from the Latin word 'granatus' which may be a reference to the malum garanatum or pomegranate. Garnet is not just one mineral but a group of related minerals, they come in all sorts of colours but the most well-known is the dark red garnet.

Garnet magical properties

Organisation, warrior spirit, protection, love, commitment, passion, sexuality, sensuality, attraction, depression, spiritual healing, success, self-confidence, energy, inspiration, perception, strength, survival, fear, courage, clarity, challenges, past life work, truth, compassion, deflecting negative energy, gossip, ambition, motivation, goals, purification, cleansing, balance, inner strength, self-empowerment, creativity, confidence, meditation, spirit work, nightmares, journeying, abundance, support

Energy:	Projective
Element:	Fie
Planet:	Mars
Zodiac:	Aries, Virgo, Capricorn, Leo, Aquarius
Birthstone:	January

Use in reflecting and deflecting spells, it will work for negative energy, lies and gossip.

Wear garnet during ritual or spell working to boost your energy.

Place garnet in your office to increase your business success.

A good stone to work with to increase your energy, particularly in the bed room department...

Suggested cleansing

Cleanse under running water, give it plenty of time to release and then put with other quartz crystals to recharge.

Garnet divination meaning

Come on shake it up, look at the mess in here, your life needs some organisation and be quick about it! Garnet brings order to chaos, it helps you get everything ship shape and in turn having organisation in your life will allow the lovely calm, refreshing, revitalised (and smug) energy to wash over you...come on, what are you sitting there for, get started!

Goldstone

Now I know this isn't a naturally occurring stone and it is in fact man made from glass with copper flecks in, but it is beautiful, and I use it regularly to work successful magic with. The story behind it tells of monks messing about with alchemy in an attempt to create gold, they knocked over a pot of copper shavings that fell into molten glass et voila goldstone was made! The original name for goldstone was 'aventurine glass' taken from the Italian word 'aventurine' which translates as 'accidental'. Goldstone is usually recognised as being brown with gold flecks, but you can also find the stone in blue with the same gold flecks. Either way it is a very pretty stone.

Goldstone magical properties

Ambition, luck, goals, determination, persistence, achievements, success, calm, emotions, energy, enthusiastic, confidence, self-belief, inner self, personal development, possibilities, courage, direction, clarity, uplifting, optimism, protection, deflects negative energy, knowledge, perception, manifestation, creativity, faith, energy flow, spirituality, abundance, wealth, grounding, perspective, ambition, drive, ingenuity, money, generosity, willpower, goals, emotions, divination (see also copper for additional magical properties).

Energy:	Receptive/Projective
Element:	Fire, Earth
Planet:	Jupiter, Venus
Zodiac:	Sagittarius

Keep goldstone in your home to bring about a calm and positive environment.

Place goldstone at work to increase productivity and creativity, it also brings in business and prosperity.

Recommend cleansing

Cleanse in lukewarm water with dish/washing up liquid soap, rinse in lukewarm water and wipe with a soft cloth. Be careful not to scratch the surface.

Goldstone divination meaning

Goldstone is the ambition stone, so this says to you, whatever you have been pondering about, whichever life pathway has been tempting you – do it. Get up off your butt and put things in motion to start reaching out for those goals that you have always dreamed of. There has never been a better time than now. Reach for the stars.

Hematite

This is a weird one and actually one of the stones that I don't work with very often as I find it very 'heavy' and overpowering, but it is excellent to use in magic. The outside is a silvery black metallic colour and the inside is stained dark red, like blood. Hematite being made mostly of iron the red colour is caused by rust. And now it gets a bit confusing...what you often find sold as hematite is in reality a stone called hematine. Hematine is made from a mixture of stainless steel, comium and nickel sulphides. It is to the eye virtually identical to natural hematite, however hematine is magnetic and natural hematite is not.

Hematite magical properties

Grounding, money, decisions, manifestation, finances, healing, focus, clarity, stability, protection, balance, divination, problem solving, emotions, self-esteem, productivity, doubt, anxiety, communication, strength

Energy:	Projective
Element:	Fire, Earth
Planet:	Saturn
Zodiac:	Aries, Aquarius

Use a piece of polished hematite as a scrying stone.

Hematite when worn by a Scorpio is said to change temperature to warn of danger.

Place in your home to dispel negative energy, preferably near doorways or windows.

Carry with you when going into a difficult situation, it will provide you with protective 'armour'.

Problems with spirits not leaving your house? Place hematite in your home to get rid of negative spiritual entities.

Keep a piece of hematite under your pillow to help you sleep and keep nightmares at bay.

Suggested cleansing

Do not cleanse with water, as it can be damaging to the stone. Cleanse with other quartz crystals or with salt. You can also use hematite to cleanse other crystals.

Hematite divination meaning

Keep your feet on the ground. Hematite says perhaps you have your head in the clouds and are away with the fairies. Much as it can be an interesting experience to chat with fairies on occasion, you really don't want to tie yourself into their world forever. Time for some proper earth, feet in the mud grounding to bring you back to reality and focus on the matters at hand. Yep, I know it sounds a bit boring snoring, but these things have to be done.

Howlite

Named after a 19th century mineralogist, Henry How, howlite is naturally a white stone with grey and black veins. However, it is a soft stone and can therefore be easily dyed so you may come across it in shades of blue or red. Howlite is a hydrous calcium borate that when in natural form is found looking like a cauliflower head with lots of nodules.

Howlite magical properties

Understanding, wisdom, connection, truth, meditation, focus, stress, anxiety, calm, strength, peace, releasing, emotions, selfishness, communication, creativity, inspiration, motivation, concentration, support, patience, relaxation, courage, past life work, astral travel

Howlite spell work

Keep a piece of howlite in your pocket to absorb negative energies that come your way or that you have yourself.

Meditate with howlite to help journey, astral travel and past life exploration.

Energy:	Projective
Element:	Earth
Planet:	Moon, Earth
Zodiac:	Gemini, Virgo

Suggested cleansing

Howlite is a soft stone so treat with care. Cleanse with lukewarm water and soap, dry with a soft cloth. If your howlite is dyed do not immerse in soapy water, cleanse with visualisation, sound, submerged in dry rice or incense smoke. Charge in the moonlight.

Howlite divination meaning

Be aware, keep those eyes, ears and your mind open. This isn't necessarily a warning, but it could be. Not everything is always as it seems. Howlite reminds you to just be aware of situations and issues around you, don't get drawn into things that don't concern you but keep an eye on your own front door step.

Jade (Nephrite)

Jade falls into the silicates category and covers jadeite and nephrite. Jade is the aggregate of either one or both of the two other minerals jadeite and nephrite. I am going to focus on nephrite as it is the easiest and cheapest to obtain, unless you are a Chinese Emperor...Nephrite is a silicate of calcium and magnesium and comes in shades of cream through green.

Jade magical properties

Purification, harmony, friendship, luck, protection, clarity, manifestation, peace, courage, wealth, longevity, wisdom, prosperity, love, renewal, fertility, uplifting, calming, confidence, truth, psychic abilities, spirit work, dreams, past life work, healing, abundance, finances, creativity, manifestation, emotions

Energy:	Receptive
Element:	Water
Planet:	Venus, Neptune
Zodiac:	Pisces, Libra, Gemini, Taurus, Aries
Birthstone:	March

A stone of love, dreams and also protection.

Suggested cleansing

Cleanse under running water, dry with a soft cloth. Do not submerge in liquid as it is porous. Don't leave out in direct sunlight as this can fade the colour. Charge with amethyst geodes or clusters.

Jade divination meaning

Make it so! Jade will help you get your finances in shape and the money rolling in. It brings the power of good luck and fortune to your doorstep.

Jasper

There are all sorts of different colours and patterns of jasper, it is a real pick n mix type of stone each piece coming in a different colour and pattern. Usually a brown base colour it also comes in other colours such as green, blue, white and red. It can be found with spots, stripes, rings and a mottled effect (in case you need a stone for camouflage this would be the one). The name translates as 'spotted or speckled' (no originality there then) and comes either from the Latin 'iaspidem' or the old French word 'jaspre'. With a base of chalcedony, it has other minerals within that give it the patterned appearance.

Jasper magical properties

General: Protection, balance, stability, healing, grounding, stress, peace, happiness, confidence, fears, comfort, relaxation, release, beauty, astral travel, motivation, determination, energy, focus, prosperity, organisation, honesty, trust

Zodiac:	Scorpio, Aries, Virgo
Birthstone:	August

Red & brick jasper

Energy:	Projective
Element:	Fire
Planet:	Mars

Guardian, protective, defensive magic, deflecting negative

energy, health, healing, beauty, transformation, balance, stability

Green jasper

Energy:	Receptive
Element:	Earth
Planet:	Venus

Healing, sleep, emotions, empathy, compassion

Brown jasper

Energy:	Projective
Element:	Air
Planet:	Mercury

Protection, grounding, control

Black jasper

Energy:	Projective
Element:	Fire
Planet:	Uranus

Personal space, protection, ritual, invisibility

Grey jasper

Energy:	Receptive
Element:	Air
Planet:	Moon

Personal power, balance, spirituality

Have jasper around your home to promote peace, harmony and balance.

Put a piece of jasper in the south west of your home to keep love in your marriage (or attract love into your life).

A good stone to carry with you for protection when travelling.

Suggested cleansing

Cleanse under warm running water and recharge by placing

with hematite stones.

Jasper divination meaning

Beauty is in the eye of the beholder and beauty comes from within. Seriously you are beautiful trust me, well trust jasper. This stone will help you see all the beautiful things about you from the outside to the inside. See your own wonderful inner light and watch it shine.

Kyanite

An aluminium silicate mineral, kyanite is usually translucent with a pearly sheen. Although found in a variety of colours the most common is blue. Translated from the Greek 'kyanos' it means 'deep blue'. No big surprise there then...

Kyanite magical properties

Balance, harmony, calming, connection, psychic abilities, healing, communication, grounding, transformation, meditation, relaxation, luck, growth, leadership, new beginnings, clarity, decisions, stability, truth, vitality, abundance, spirituality, channelling, understanding, dreams

Energy:	Receptive
Element:	Water
Planet:	Jupiter, Venus, Mars
Zodiac:	Aries, Libra, Taurus

Place kyanite in the east or south east of your home to bring in prosperity.

Suggested cleansing

Kyanite does not hold onto negative energy, it is self-cleansing. It can be used to cleanse other crystals too. Charge with other quartz crystals if you feel it needs a boost.

Kyanite divination meaning

Sit down, shut up and take a chill pill. Honestly calm down, coz you aren't doing anyone any good in this chaotic state. Kyanite asks you to just breathe…take a step back and look at the big picture, what have you been doing and how have you been reacting? Ground and centre yourself and take a fresh look.

Labradorite

Labradorite (always makes me think of a happy dog…) although the name apparently has nothing to do with Labrador dogs but comes from the place it was first discovered which was Labrador in Canada. It is part of the feldspar group of minerals, those that are aluminium silicates containing potassium, sodium and/or calcium. Feldspar minerals are the most abundant group of mineral stones. Labradorite is often associated with moonstone, the structure being similar with moonstone being the lighter energy and labradorite carrying the darker. By that I don't mean good and evil, labradorite just seems to work with more inner energy, think Crone magic.

Labradorite magical properties

Transformation, cleansing, breaking patterns, potential, psychic abilities, intuition, confidence, spirituality, focus, protection, imagination, relaxation, soothing, energy, healing, stress, anxiety, luck, abundance, success, decisions, trust, changes, strength, courage, self-confidence, inspiration, perseverance, journeying, clarity, insight, meditation, depression, jealousy, grounding

Energy:	Projective
Element:	Water
Planet:	Earth, Moon, Uranus
Zodiac:	Aquarius, Sagittarius, Scorpio, Leo

Wear labradorite to combat jealousy and allow negative energy to bounce away from you.

Use labradorite to help with astral projection.

Labradorite is a stone of magic and helps awaken that power from within, it raises your consciousness and helps you connect with energy around you, wear when working any type of magic or in ritual.

Suggested cleansing

Cleanse under running water and recharge in moonlight.

Labradorite divination meaning

A time of transition is upon you, don't fight it, open your arms wide and embrace it. Labradorite will help you awaken your own magic and provide clarity and insight to allow you to find the 'true you'. It will take you on a journey of self-discovery providing courage and confidence with each turn of the pathway. Enjoy the magic!

Lapis lazuli

Sounds like the baddie from a James Bond film...it is however a very beautiful and magical stone. Lapis lazuli is composed of the mineral lazurite with added bits and bobs such as calcite and spots of pyrite. The fancy name disappointingly has a boring meaning, it comes from Latin with 'lapis' translating as 'stone' and some say from the Persian word 'lazhward' meaning blue, others suggest it is from the Arabic word 'aula' which also means blue. Whatever way, basically it is a blue stone. The Ancient Egyptians used lapis lazuli in cosmetics and many Renaissance artists used it in their paint, presumably ground up and not in whole lumps...

Lapis lazuli magical properties

Protection, manifestation, meditation, psychic protection,

problem solving, knowledge, clarity, decisions, memory, spirituality, peace, energy, organisation, concentration, stress, luck, negative energy, wealth, abundance, success, love, confidence, truth, renewal, intellect, wisdom, leadership, legal issues, sleep, anxiety, harmony, understanding

Energy:	Receptive
Element:	Water
Planet:	Venus, Jupiter
Zodiac:	Sagittarius

Place lapis lazuli in the south east of your home or office to bring in the money.

For promotion place a piece in the north side of your office.

Put some in the east of your home to bring good health.

Lapis is a really mental stone, not as in 'mad as a bucket of frogs' but as in helping you focus and organise your thoughts.

Suggested cleansing

Lapis lazuli is quite a delicate stone and can chip or crack easily if knocked.

The stone is also slightly porous, so I would avoid cleaning agents.

Cleanse with incense smoke or visualisation and charge under the starry skies.

Lapis lazuli divination meaning

Find the truth of the matter. Don't listen to gossip, go to the source and seek out the facts rather than the fiction that everyone likes to create around an issue or event. Lapis lazuli will help you don your deer stalker cap and Sherlock out the details. Don't believe everything you hear or see, it is easy to be deceived sometimes by your own heart and mind. The truth will be liberating.

Larimar

A pretty bluey/green variety of pectolite, this is sometimes referred to as 'The Atlantis stone'. Discovered apparently in the early 1900s by a Spanish priest but no action was taken, it was re-discovered in the 1970s by a Peace Corp chap named Mendez who called it after his daughter Lari 'Larisa' and 'mar' being the Spanish word for 'sea'. The stone is believed to have volcanic beginnings.

Larimar magical properties

Peace, clarity, healing, inspiration, spirituality, understanding, calming, soothing, uplifting, emotions, fears, depression, patience, creativity, love, communication, friendship, guidance, happiness, decisions, relaxation, meditation, wisdom, divine, harmony

Energy:	Receptive
Element:	Water/Fire/Spirit
Planet:	Neptune
Zodiac:	Pisces

Suggested cleansing

Keep out of sunlight as it can be damaging to larimar. Cleanse with warm water and a soft cloth.

Larimar divination meaning

This can set you free...Let go of anything that worries you, pack up your troubles, leave your cares behind and set yourself free. Fly...

Lepidolite

A form of mica lepidolite is source of lithium. It is made from layers of hexagonal plates, aluminium silicate sheets bound with layers of potassium ions. Found in shades of purple through to pink it sometimes has crystal lines through it.

Lepidolite magical properties
Transformation, soothing, calming, stress, happiness, changes, emotions, psychic abilities, spirituality, depression, divination, connection, strength, uplifting, luck, hope, balance, peace, sleep, harmony, decisions, addiction, releasing, trust, goals, optimism, patience, dreams, opportunities, support, love

Energy:	Receptive
Element:	Water
Planet:	Jupiter, Neptune
Zodiac:	Libra

Lepidolite spell work
Keep lepidolite beside your bed to enhance your dreams and bring about a calm energy.

Pop a piece of lepidolite in your home or office to create a happy and calm environment.

Suggested cleansing
Lepidolite is a soft stone so be careful as it can be easily damaged.

Cleanse with incense smoke or visualisation.

Lepidolite divination meaning
Time for a bit of de-stressing. Life can throw us lemons, oranges, limes and all kinds of fruit at any given time. How we deal with it is the important part. I know it is easy to say but getting stressed ain't gonna help ya none. Step back, take a deep breath and calmly and critically assess the situation. What can you do to help yourself? Getting all stressed up and anxious is only going to make things worse. Make time, take time, do what is right for you.

Malachite

A breath-taking green stone usually with green bands and green rings running through/around it (basically green with more green). The green is caused by copper. This one is ancient and the history of it being used goes back thousands of years. Worn by the ancient Egyptians and Greeks for various magical uses such as protective talismans, on headdresses and used for healing. It has even been used to decorate the inside of grand houses. The name derives from the Greek word 'malakos' which translates as 'soft'. Although personally I think it needs a name that translates to mean 'green'... It is said that malachite can warn of danger by breaking into pieces.

Malachite magical properties

Changes, transformation, clarity, emotions, protection, support, healing, peace, travel, fears, growth, creativity, renewal, energy, wealth, money, opportunity, abundance, new beginnings, finances, success, business, focus, strength, wisdom, releasing, prosperity, breaking barriers, psychic abilities, manifestation, soothing, stress, love, power

Energy:	Receptive
Element:	Earth
Planet:	Venus
Zodiac:	Capricorn, Scorpio

Tell a piece of malachite all about your fears and worries then take the malachite and place it outside overnight to allow it to remove your concerns.

Place a piece of malachite on the dining room table to increase appetites and help fussy eaters.

For prosperity pop a piece of malachite in the south east or east of your house.

To increase the energy flow in your office or home place a

piece of malachite in the blocked area.

Keep a piece of malachite next to your computer or any electric appliances to protect you from any harmful energy.

Use malachite to draw out any bad habits or break destructive patterns.

Malachite is a stone of magic and will give an extra oomph of power and energy to most magical workings including rituals and divination.

Suggested cleaning

Be careful with malachite, it can be easily damaged. Don't expose it to extreme or sudden changes in temperature. Cleanse amongst other quartz crystals or place in the soil.

Malachite divination meaning

Express yourself. Malachite encourages you to take a look at your own thoughts and actions and claim responsibility for them. It will help you to see both sides of any situation and view it with understanding and empathy. Allowing you then to express your own true thoughts on the matter but from a sensible and balance viewpoint.

Moonstone

The light side of labradorite, moonstone is a member of the feldspar group, an alkali feldspar to be precise. The beautiful sheen that the moonstone has is called 'adularescence' and is caused by structural anomalies (albite) within the crystal formation (I think the Star Trek Enterprise went there once...). Obviously this one has a very strong connection to the moon carrying a powerful feminine energy, so it works well for any kind of goddess or female directed magic.

Moonstone magical properties

New beginnings, moon magic, intuition, calming, psychic

abilities, balance, harmony, wishes, cleansing, uplifting, hope, meditation, emotions, love, divination, spirituality, wealth, truth, healing, sensuality, insight, peace, wisdom, communication, confidence, abundance, prosperity, dreams, fertility, travel

Energy:	Receptive
Element:	Water
Planet:	Moon
Zodiac:	Cancer, Libra, Scorpio
Birthstone:	June, September

Moonstone can be used instead of a pearl in magical workings.

Use on the waning moon for divination and on the waxing moon for love spells.

Work with moonstone to decide what moon phase it works best for you on, it may differ depending on how you attune to the phases.

Wear moonstone or place a piece on the table when working with divination, it will increase your connection and psychic abilities.

Place a piece in the south west, west or north west of your home to bring in love and happiness.

Carry with you for protection when you travel.

Suggested cleansing
Cleanse among other quartz crystals or hematite. Charge under the moonlight.

Moonstone divination meaning
Use your intuition, not only use it but trust in it, your inner instincts will never be wrong. Learn to trust your gut feelings. If it feels hinky then it probably is, if it feels good, go with it.

Obsidian (black)

This has got to be one of the most 'heavy metal' gemstones as it is formed from volcanic lava (you can throw horns and head bang with this one). Because of it being made from volcanic glass it carries the properties of fire, water and earth. The use of obsidian for tools and spear points goes back to prehistoric man. Obsidian comes in our favourite colour...black. Although you can also find obsidian in a reddy brown which is called mahogany obsidian, a silica rich volcanic rock with darker flecks of hematit. And with white flecks which is snowflake obsidian, still volcanic glass but with white splodges of phenocryst. Obsidian has the wonderful ability to absorb negative energy and transform it into positive.

Obsidian magical properties

Truth, healing, clarity, illusions, breaking barriers, integrity, grounding, centring, strength, courage, protection, cleansing, meditation, stress, calming, relaxation, depression, anxiety, wealth, luck, focus, emotions, power, determination, success, patience, perseverance, releasing, spirit work, spirituality, challenges, past life work, divination

Energy:	Projective
Element:	Fire, Earth, Water
Planet:	Saturn, Jupiter
Zodiac:	Sagittarius

A perfect stone for divination and prophesy.

Obsidian is brilliant to work with for protection and to dispel negative energy.

A really good crystal to help you release that which no longer serves you and to let go of old patterns.

Suggested cleansing

Cleanse by running under lukewarm water or under the sun or moonlight.

Obsidian divination meaning

Obsidian asks, "Are you being totally honest with yourself?" Allow this stone to help you clear blockages and take off those rose-tinted glasses and see yourself and your situation as it truly is. This is not a time to be delicate, pull on your big girl or boy panties and take a serious look. It is all about being truly honest about how you are behaving and where you are headed.

Pebble/Hag stone

I wanted to include the humble pebble or hag/holey stone. If you have a river or a beach nearby you can find all sorts of beautiful natural stones, pebbles and even on occasion hag stones (a pebble with a hole in). Each pebble will be created from a mixture of minerals. These stones although not considered to be crystals still pack a powerful punch of magic. If found in a field they will have a strong earth energy. Pebbles from the beach or river bed will have that same earth magic but with water added in as well. Holey/hag stones can be held up to your eye so that you can see things in the Otherworld or Fairy realm.

Pebble/hag stone magical properties

Protection, fairy magic, nightmares, dreams, healing, fertility, manifestation, negative energy

Energy:	Projective
Element:	Earth, Water
Planet:	Earth

Suggested cleansing

Cleanse in running under water or under the sun or moonlight.

Pebble divination meaning

This stone brings a mix of Earth and Water energy so it either brings a nice balance, with you keeping your emotions in check whilst using your sensible head. Or it can be saying "seriously stop with the emo stuff and use your brain!". Which one does it signify? If it is the former then take a pat on the back, otherwise you might need to get your act together to be able to move forward.

Petrified wood

This is one of those stones that isn't a stone and also one with a really unimaginative name...'petrified wood' comes from the Greek word 'petro' which means 'stone' so it is pretty much called 'wood turned into stone'. It is actually just that, the fossilised remains of vegetation, a tree that has turned into stone. The silicate minerals replace the original organic material of the tree but keep the same structure. The silicate is often quartz and the colour of the stone comes from elements such as copper, iron and manganese that are present in the mud or water as the material petrifies. There is a joke here about being scared but nothing comes to mind at the moment...

Petrified wood magical properties

Stability, grounding, calming, anxiety, fears, meditation, determination, decisions, strength, courage, patience, transformation, perseverance, success, luck, emotions, wisdom, past life work, insight, leadership

Energy:	Receptive
Element:	Earth, Spirit
Planet:	Earth, Sun
Zodiac:	All

Carry a piece of petrified wood with you or place in your home to help you feel connected to nature.

Recommend cleansing

Cleanse with incense smoke or place with quartz crystals. Charge by placing in nature.

Petrified wood divination meaning

Keep your feet firmly on the ground and look to your family and friends that surround you. Support and stability can be found right at your feet, or at least in your local area. Don't cast your net too wide, seek out the help or a listening ear closer to home.

Pyrite

Pyrite has the common name 'fool's gold' and is a disulfide of iron. It often forms into shapes such as cubes and flat discs. The name is derived from the Greek word 'pyr' which means 'fire'. The fool's gold name is a bit mean to be honest, it does look like gold, but this stone is definitely no fool. Some ancient cultures would make scrying mirrors from pyrite, polishing one side flat to use for divination and carving symbols into the reverse side. It has also been used throughout history for healing, protective amulets and adornments.

Pyrite magical properties

Releasing, breaking patterns, clarity, protection, support, decisions, growth, success, inspiration, grounding, vitality, learning, perception, memory, wisdom, psychic abilities, healing, cleansing, prosperity, wealth, abundance, luck, strength, motivation, manifestation, finances, energy, sun magic, power, focus, perseverance, confidence, divination, communication, self-confidence, meditation

Energy:	Projective
Element:	Fire

Planet:	Mars, Sun
Zodiac:	Leo

A brilliant stone to increase your creativity and really get your imagination working overtime.

Suggested cleansing

Pyrite is brittle and can shatter quite easily. Do not put pyrite in water.

Cleanse with salt or incense smoke. Recharge under the sunlight but don't leave it out too long or pop next to quartz crystals.

Pyrite divination meaning

Oooh shiny gold things...pyrite brings wealth and abundance your way, it also opens up doors and opportunities for you to earn money and bring cash flowing into your life. Keep an eye open for them. But don't be fooled into thinking you can throw it around all at once, budget and be careful how you spend it.

Quartz (clear)

Probably one of the most common and well known of crystals, the quartz is such a useful, good all-round stone. This stone is a 'jack of all trades' and actually really is a master of all of them too. Quartz crystal is made from silicon dioxide. They sometimes have other minerals in the, creating shadows or shapes and making them rutilated. Double ended clear quartz and quartz points are often used as 'master healers' being able to channel illness and pain out from the body. It is a very powerful stone and can also be used to cleanse other crystals. The name 'quartz' is from the Greek word 'krustallos' which translates as 'ice'. It was believed that the Gods created it and people believed it to be ice.

Quartz magical properties

Purification, cleansing, healing, calming, emotions, strength, support, spirituality, energy, balance, psychic abilities, motivation, uplifting, decisions, anxiety, divine connection, amplifying, focus, meditation, manifestation, channelling, protection, negative energy, clarity, wisdom, concentration, learning, spirit work, communication, astral travel, divination, dreams, harmony

Energy:	Projective, Receptive
Planet:	Sun, Moon
Element:	Fire, Water
Zodiac:	Leo, Gemini, Capricorn

Use a quartz point to direct energy to your intent in spell work.

If you only ever use one crystal, make it this one. It is so versatile and can be charged and programmed for pretty much anything.

Suggested cleansing

Cleanse with running water, incense smoke or visualisation, you can also cleanse quartz in a bowl of dried rice or a mixture of dried flower petals and herbs. Quartz also responds well to cleansing with crystal bowls or bells. Charge under the moonlight, sunlight or bury in the soil.

Quartz divination meaning

As quartz is a master healer stone perhaps it is telling you that you need to take some time for yourself? Running around and trying to do everything for everyone one all at once will drain you, if it hasn't done so already. It really is OK to say 'no' sometimes. You cannot keep up a full-on pace if your stores are depleted. Please take care of yourself first before you continue...

Quartz (Rose)

For me, rose quartz is a very gentle, calm energy and most definitely one filled with love. It really is a stone of the heart and all matters attached to it. But don't be fooled, just because the energy is gentle it does pack a powerful punch of magic. The base of the stone is quartz, but the colour is created by impurities such as titanium, manganese and iron.

Rose quartz magical properties

Love, happiness, emotions, spirituality, growth, fears, healing, sexuality, passion, calming, soothing, stress, depression, sleep, luck, wisdom, inspiration, success, intuition, grounding, balance, prosperity, self-esteem, harmony, trust, jealousy, gossip, beauty, peace, cleansing, fertility

Energy:	Receptive
Element:	Earth, Water
Planet:	Venus, Moon
Zodiac:	Taurus

Place a piece of rose quartz in your purse or wallet to attract money.

Pop a piece of rose quartz in the far-right corner of your home to bring love and happiness in.

Rose quartz is a love stone but particularly for self-love and friendships.

Work with rose quartz for emotions and all matters of the heart.

Suggested cleansing

Cleanse regularly under lukewarm running water. Quartz can also be cleansed by placing it next to an amethyst or another quartz crystal. Don't place in the sunlight as it can fade. Charge in moonlight.

Rose quartz divination meaning

Love is in the air...la la la la laaaaa. This stone is bringing you all that smushy, romantic lurve stuff. It arrives with red roses, chocolates and a big ole bottle of bubbly, dressed James Bond style. There can be no mistaking this ooh la la kissy energy coming your way. Whether it is new love on the horizon or a rekindling of an old flame or perhaps a bit of a kick up the butt for your current relationship, better put your best underwear on...

Quartz (smoky)

The base of this stone is obviously quartz which is silicone dioxide, but the dark smoky colour comes from free silicone deposits within the stone. Apparently in 12th Century China the first sunglasses were made, using pieces of smoky quartz as the lenses, very clever.

Smoky quartz magical properties

Grounding, centring, focus, negative energy, decisions, cooperation, creativity, emotions, depression, anxiety, jealousy, nature, protection, calming, manifestation, wishes, divination, meditation, insight, guidance, uplifting, fears, relaxation, releasing, abundance, luck, prosperity

Energy:	Receptive
Element:	Earth
Planet:	Saturn, Jupiter
Zodiac:	Capricorn, Sagittarius

Place smoky quartz around your home in any areas where the energy feels hinky.

Keep a piece of smoky quartz next to your computer to absorb any bad energy.

Smoky quartz is brilliant to help you ground but it also guides you in business success.

Suggested cleansing

Smoky quartz can scratch and chip easily so be gentle with it. Cleanse with water and a small amount of soap, dry with a soft cloth. Don't soak your quartz in water and don't leave it out in the sun, it will fade. Charge in moonlight.

Smoky quartz divination meaning

Problems come in all shapes and sizes and usually when we least expect them. Smoky quartz can help you sort out the facts, take a step back and see the situation with clarity and to come up with various options to solve the issue. Think logically and weigh up the different avenues available to you, smoky quartz will help you make the right decision.

Rhodochrosite

A really pretty pink and pearly white stone, looks good enough to eat (don't though, seriously don't). The name derives from the Greek word 'rhodos' which translates as 'rose' and 'khros' which is 'colour', so pretty simple really, 'rose colour'. The beautiful pink colour comes from manganese which combines with a carbonate material. The Incas believed that the crystal was the spilt blood of their rulers.

Rhodochrosite magical properties

Power, potential, strength, confidence, healing, new beginnings, breaking barriers, releasing, joy, happiness, creativity, determination, manifestation, prosperity, abundance, love, emotions, peace, renewal, connection, balance, spirituality, harmony, energy

Energy:	Projective
Element:	Fire

Planet: Mars, Jupiter
Zodiac: Scorpio, Leo

To connect with a person, place a piece of rhodochrosite next to their photograph and say their name three times.

Add a piece of rhodochrosite to your bathwater for a relaxing and de-stressing bathe.

Pop a piece of rhodochrosite and some rose petals into your bath and light pink candles whilst focusing on drawing love to you for a powerful love spell.

Suggested cleansing

As a fairly soft stone it can scratch easily, treat with care. Cleanse with soapy water, rinse and dry with a soft cloth. Charge in moonlight.

Rhodochrosite divination meaning

One of the keys to a successful life is getting the balance right, and it ain't always easy, trust me, I know. Rhodochrosite asks that you take a look at the balance in your own life. Are you weighted too much on work and not enough on family, friends or home life? Having that unbalance in your life can cause you any amount of distress. It won't necessarily be easy but see if you can readjust the scales, even just a tiny bit at first. Make small changes to begin with and start to even things up a bit. You will reap the benefits from it.

Rhodonite

A beautiful pink stone shot through with dark veins, it is a silicate/quartz composite with the pink colour being created by manganese and the dark lines are impurities of black manganese oxide and dendrite. The name derives from the Greek word 'rhodos' which translates as 'rose'.

Rhodonite magical properties

Protection, renewal, emotions, strength, soothing, clarity, happiness, love, balance, harmony, decisions, confidence, spirituality, peace, energy, passion, optimism, changes, vitality, anxiety, travel, psychic abilities, self-confidence, trust, calming, relaxation, patience, determination, releasing, stress, negative energy

Energy:	Projective
Element:	Fire
Planet:	Mars, Venus
Zodiac:	Taurus

Rhodonite absorbs negative energy from around you so it is very effective to keep in your home or office.

This is 'the' stone for anyone that loves music and will help you to listen and learn.

Work with rhodonite to help overcome loss or grief.

Suggested cleansing

Cleanse with incense smoke or bury in the soil and recharge under moonlight. Rhodonite can also be cleansed by placing next to selenite.

Rhodonite divination meaning

Harmony is another one of life's sometimes seemingly elusive states to find. If you can bring about balance in your life, work and home you will find that harmony and peace follow suit. You have the power...

Selenite

The name means 'moonstone' and was possibly named after the Greek moon goddess, Selene. It is a beautiful ethereal crystal and is a form of gypsum, often created as seawater evaporates.

Selenite magical properties

Clarity, psychic protection, cleansing, balance, stability, emotions, divine, connections, spirituality, psychic abilities, spirit work, protection, healing, breaking barriers, decisions, intuition, meditation, money, success, love

Energy:	Receptive
Element:	Water
Planet:	Moon
Zodiac:	Cancer

Place selenite in each of the four corners of your home to bring peace in.

Pop a piece of selenite under your pillow to help get a good night's sleep.

Can you hear the harps playing? This is 'the' divine connection crystal.

Suggested cleansing

Do not cleanse in water, it can be very damaging to selenite. Cleanse with visualisation or sound such as a crystal or singing bowl. Charge in the moonlight.

Selenite can be used to cleanse and charge other crystals.

Selenite divination meaning

Selenite is one of the most spiritual crystals going so if this appears in your reading perhaps it is reminding you of your spirituality? Have you lost your connection? When was the last time you did something spiritual? Meditated even? Selenite is here to give you a nudge to jump back on the magical band wagon and relight your spiritual fire.

Serpentine

A group of green crystals, the name may refer to the stone

colouring resembling that of a snake. It is either a leafy pattern, being antigorite or a fibrous one, which is chrysotile. The crystals you will find in the shops are antigorite, as the chrysotile type contains asbestos fibres. Romans liked to use serpentine as a protection against dark magic. Serpentine was thought to break if it came into contact with poison. This crystal is actually quite fire resistant too.

Serpentine magical properties

Meditation, peace, clarity, nature, fairy magic, emotions, calming, protection, negative energy, love, prosperity, manifestation, psychic protection, success, cleansing

Energy:	Projective
Element:	Fire
Planet:	Saturn
Zodiac:	Gemini

Life in a shambles and everything falling apart? Call upon the magic of serpentine to bring it all back together, order from chaos.

Suggested cleansing

Serpentine is quite a soft, fragile stone so treat carefully. Cleanse with warm water and a soft cloth.

Serpentine divination meaning

This stone brings the power of the serpent that inner strength that lies dormant until really provoked. Draw on that base energy and use it to the full extent, you are within your rights to protect yourself and those you love.

Sodalite

Royal blue in colour and often with white specks or streaks

of calcite in, the main fabric of this gemstone is sodium. The name may be derived from the element name of sodium but also the Latin word 'sodalitas' which translates as 'comrade' which echoes the properties of the stone. It is a creative stone and one often favoured by artists and writers.

Sodalite magical properties

Creativity, communication, peace, friendship, clarity, truth, connection, knowledge, wisdom, emotions, balance, divination, psychic abilities, cleansing, confidence, fears, love, intuition, decisions, perseverance, anxiety, insight, organisation, self-esteem, releasing, understanding, harmony, learning, dreams, meditation

Energy:	Receptive
Element:	Water
Planet:	Jupiter, Venus
Zodiac:	Sagittarius

Suggested cleansing

Sodalite can be fragile so handle carefully. Do not immerse in water, it may lose its shine, but cleansing can be done under a short burst of lukewarm running water. Alternatively cleanse with incense smoke, visualisation or sound. Charge in the moonlight or with crystal quartz stones.

Sodalite divination meaning

Get yer paints and crayons out coz it's time to get creative! OK, it might not actually mean finger painting pictures of dinosaurs (rawr!) as creativity covers more than artistic talents. It might mean you restart that journal that you left collecting dust or get into the kitchen and bake. It may just mean you ought to try being a bit more creative with the way you look at the world...

Sugilite

This stone has a really bright purple 1980's vibe to it...without the leg warmers. The colour comes from manganese. The stone was discovered in Japan during the 40s by a geologist called Ken-ichi-Sugi hence the name 'sugilite'. It is an excellent stone to work with for any kind of spiritual growth and spirituality.

Sugilite magical properties

Spirituality, wisdom, clarity, insight, courage, truth, passion, inspiration, healing, strength, channelling, psychic abilities, amplification, confidence, focus, love, emotions, releasing, calming, peace, protection, connection, balance, understanding, stress

Energy:	Receptive
Element:	Water
Planet:	Mercury, Jupiter
Zodiac:	Virgo

Keep a piece of sugilite under your pillow to cleanse, heal and protect your personal energy while you sleep.

Sugilite will help you understand how your thoughts and ideas affect your physical body (not sure I want to know...).

Suggested cleansing

Sugilite is super charged all the time so it is recommended that you discharge it regularly by cleansing next to hematite stones.

Sugilite divination meaning

This stone is all about connecting the spiritual to the physical and helping you understand 'the all'. It packs a powerful punch of spiritual energy and one that asks you to really work on your inner spirit. Let go of that which doesn't serve you and allow yourself to move onwards and upwards into your full and true spiritual potential.

Sunstone

Sunstone is part of the feldspar family of stones usually an orange colour with a sparkle caused by inclusions of hematite or pyrite. Sunstone was prized by ancient civilisations as they believed it to be a piece of the sun fallen to earth.

Sunstone magical properties

Sun magic, power, decisions, leadership, strength, happiness, inspiration, love, luck, stability, clarity, energy, stress, depression, emotions, optimism, perseverance, intuition, fears, self-esteem, self-confidence, healing, balance, harmony, abundance, prosperity, opportunities, peace, protection

Energy:	Projective
Element:	Fire
Planet:	Sun
Zodiac:	Leo

For a perfect pairing and balance of energy keep a sunstone and a moonstone together.

Suggested cleansing

Sprinkle with salt or drop into a glass of salt water to cleanse. Sunstone can also be cleansed in moonlight but use the waning moon phase. Don't place for long periods of time in direct sunlight it can fade the colour. Sunstone can also be cleansed by covering with dried herbs or flowers or burying in the soil.

Sunstone divination meaning

The sun has got his hat on...hip hip hip hooray! This stone brings heap loads of positive sunshiny energy. It will help you sweep through your life with a surge of bright cheerful vibes.

Tiger's Eye

Tiger's Eye is a pseudomorph (definitely saw him in Star Trek) which is a mineral that chemically replaces another mineral without changing the external form of the original mineral. It forms when quartz takes over and dissolves crocidolite leaving behind the brown and gold stripy form we are familiar with. The name of the stone came from...the fact it looks like the eye of a tiger, or a cat. It has long been believed to be an all seeing and all-knowing kinda gem.

Tiger's eye magical properties

Amplification, balance, harmony, releasing, fears, anxiety, courage, strength, self-confidence, focus, creativity, optimism, self-worth, protection, psychic abilities, healing, wealth, money, opportunity, abundance, prosperity, luck, success, commitment, determination, support, clarity, vitality, motivation, grounding, patience

Energy:	Projective
Element:	Fire, Earth
Planet:	Sun
Zodiac:	Leo, Capricorn

Keep a piece of tiger's eye at work to bring inspiration and lots of sales.

Suggested cleansing

As Tiger's eye is a fire and earth stone cleanse using incense smoke or bury in the soil. Charge in the early morning sunlight.

Tiger's eye divination meaning

Tiger's eye brings you the strength and courage that a tiger would...rawr! Tap into the primal energy and bring that vibe into your own life. Don't sit around waiting for things to happen, get up, get going and grab 'em by the tail!

Tourmaline

A pretty stone that comes in a variety of colours, it isn't a single mineral but a group, elbaite being the one responsible for most of the varieties. The name seems to stem from a Sinhalese word 'turamali' which literally means 'stones of mixed colours'. They really need to put more effort into naming gemstones...The Ancient Egyptians believed that tourmaline travelled along a rainbow from the core of the earth up towards the sun, collecting the colours of the rainbow as it went.

Tourmaline magical properties

Calming, harmony, balance, insight, spirituality, protection, negative energy, transformation, courage, grounding, fears, creativity, understanding, power, motivation, commitment, patience, stability, releasing, emotions, anxiety, strength, happiness, protection, relaxation, friendship, astral travel

Energy:	Receptive (pink, green, blue, black, watermelon)
	Projective (watermelon, red)
Element:	Water (pink, blue, watermelon)
	Fire (watermelon, red)
	Earth (green, black)
Planet:	Venus, Mars
Zodiac:	Libra
Birthstone:	October

Work with tourmaline to release and let go. It has the ability to guide you and your emotions and re-direct that energy into all the positive good stuff.

Suggested cleansing

Tourmaline can be damaged easily, don't store it together with other stones. It also doesn't like severe temperature changes (who does?). Cleanse with water and a little soap solution, wipe dry with a soft cloth. Charge in the moonlight or with sound.

Tourmaline divination meaning

Don't worry...be happy.

Turquoise

Turquoise comes in various shades of... turquoise. It is a hydrous phosphate mineral made of aluminium and copper. Named from the French word 'turquoise' which translates as 'Turkish stone' as it arrived in Europe from Asia via Turkey. It has been used and worn as bling for centuries, the first recorded jewellery using turquoise was for the Queen Zar who ruled Egypt in 5500BC. The stone was used in Tibet as currency and valued higher than gold.

Turquoise magical properties

Purification, negative energy, protection, balance, relaxation, emotions, stress, spirituality, energy, depression, clarity, wisdom, understanding, psychic abilities, insight, intuition, past life work, communication, wealth, abundance, finances, prosperity, luck, decisions, friendship, uplifting, meditation, love, harmony

Energy:	Receptive
Element:	Earth
Planet:	Venus, Neptune
Zodiac:	Sagittarius, Pisces, Aquarius
Birthstone:	December

If it is good enough for the Pharaohs it will work for you, it can help you release negative energy and transform it all into the good stuff.

Turquoise is uplifting and inspiring.

Suggested cleansing

Turquoise is porous so be careful with liquids or oils of any kind. It is also fairly soft so treat careful to prevent scratching or chipping. Cleanse with incense smoke, visualisation or sound. Turquoise responds well to cleansing by being placed with quartz crystals or hematite.

Turquoise divination meaning

Turquoise is a stone of friendship. Remember that you are never alone and that your friends can provide you with all the support you need. Don't be afraid to reach out to them.

Unakite

Created from granite flecked with pink orthoclase feldspar, green epidote and quartz crystals. The name comes from the Unakas Mountains in the United States where it was first discovered.

Unakite magical properties

Love, happiness, growth, wealth, success, harmony, decisions, support, balance, emotions, stability, confidence, strength, anxiety, nature, courage, transformation, releasing, spirituality

Energy:	Receptive
Element:	Fire, Water
Planet:	Mars, Venus, Pluto
Zodiac:	Scorpio

Unakite works well when placed in the garden, it will bring life and growth to all your plants.

This crystal will help you leave the past behind and 'live in the now man'.

Suggested cleansing

Unakite is porous so don't use any kind of chemicals. Cleanse with a mild soap and water mix and dry with a soft cloth.

Unakite divination meaning

Unakite is a stone of unity, one of bonding together. Use that strength to your advantage whether it is with family of friends. Create a united front, together you can deal with anything that is thrown your way.

Magical metals

I know technically it isn't crystals or gems but if you wear jewellery then chances are it will be set into a metal of some kind. Each of those metals also carries magical oomph.

Silver

My personal favourite (just in case anyone wants to buy me a present…) Silver plays a supportive role to any crystal that is set into it. Most silver is created from silver ore but is often mixed with gold, antimony and arsenic (eep!). It is also a metal with the highest optical reflective quality. It is also a very good conductor of energy. The Egyptians created silver bowls for purification rituals.

Silver magical properties

Healing, communication, cleansing, energy, intuition, stability, spirituality, patience, perseverance, moon magic, negative energy, protection, balance, psychic abilities, manifestation, wealth, prosperity, abundance, travel, dreams, emotions, purification, love, peace, astral travel

Energy: Receptive

Element:	Water
Planet:	Moon
Zodiac:	Cancer

Suggested cleansing

Silver doesn't react to water or oxygen, but it does with sulphides and sulphur which cause it to tarnish. Clean with a silver polish cloth. Charge in moonlight.

Gold

Gold is a fantastic conductor of energy and therefore makes it a brilliant healer. Gold will enhance and boost the energy of any other gemstone. It has been seen over Centuries of time as a symbol of wealth, power, status and abundance.

Gold magical properties

Prosperity, action, power, healing, renewal, self-esteem, wealth, all round sunshine energy, wisdom, learning, potential, self-confidence, self-worth, calm, negative energy, transformation, spirituality, nature, happiness, energy, stress, the divine, sun magic, ritual, illumination, understanding

Energy:	Projective
Element:	Fire
Planet:	Sun
Zodiac:	Leo

Suggested cleansing

There are a lot of specialised gold cleaning solutions on the market and they will work well but so does good ole liquid dish/ washing up detergent in a bowl of lukewarm water. Soak the gold and then rinse in warm running water, dry with a soft cloth.

Copper

Definitely a healing metal it is a huge conductor of power, heat and energy that also includes spiritual energy. Copper can also be used to amplify psychic abilities and magical energy. The Egyptians were some of the first people to use copper (and tin and bronze, darn clever those Egyptians).

Copper magical properties

It provides support, co-operation, protection, love, attraction, purification, self-esteem, positive energy, communication, energy, psychic abilities, channelling, balance, understanding, harmony, money, confidence, optimism, divine connection, luck

Energy:	Receptive
Element:	Water
Planet:	Venus
Zodiac:	Taurus, Sagittarius

Suggested cleansing

Dip copper in a solution of warm water, lemon juice and salt to remove any tarnish, then rinse and dry. Tomato ketchup can also be used with a soft brush.

Brass

The love child of copper and zinc, brass is a good healer and brings a powerful punch of purification and cleansing. It also brings strength, stability, abundance, wealth and protection.

Bronze

Also, a copper and zinc baby it has the same magical properties as brass but is much better at helping you reach your goals and provides personal inner strength.

Platinum

Basically, a very expensive metal that looks like silver...in my humble opinion! However, it has a super strong energy and can overpower most crystals that are set into it.

LOTS OF LISTS...

In this section I have created correspondence lists to help when looking for the right stone to do the job. This list is by no means comprehensive! However, as I always say...trust your intuition (and your finances, or lack thereof) when choosing the stones to work with.

Intent

Abundance
Moss agate, amber, brass, calcite (orange), carnelian, citrine, garnet, goldstone, jade (nephrite), kyanite, labradorite, lapis lazuli, malachite, moonstone, pyrite, quartz (smoky), rhodochrosite, silver, sunstone, tiger's eye, turquoise

Action
Gold

Adaptability
Bloodstone

Addictions (overcoming)
Amethyst, lepidolite

Ambition
Goldstone

Amplification (of other stones or magic)
Calcite (orange), fluorite, quartz, sugilite, tiger's eye

Adventure
Aventurine (green)

Anxiety (relieving)
Amethyst, aventurine (green), bloodstone, fluorite, hematite, howlite, labradorite, lapis lazuli, obsidian (black), petrified wood, quartz, quartz (smoky), rhodonite, sodalite, tiger's eye, tourmaline, unakite

Astral travel
Celestite, howlite, jasper, quartz, silver, tourmaline

Attraction
Copper, garnet

Balance
Agate, amber, aventurine (green), chrysocolla, chrysoprase, copper, fluorite, garnet, hematite, jasper, kyanite, lepidolite, moonstone, quartz, quartz (rose), rhodochrosite, rhodonite, selenite, silver, sodalite, sugilite, sunstone, tiger's eye, tourmaline, turquoise, unakite

Beauty
Amber, jasper, quartz (rose)

Beginnings
Moss agate, kyanite, malachite, moonstone, rhodochrosite

Breaking barriers
Bloodstone, chrysoprase, malachite, obsidian (black), rhodochrosite, selenite

Breaking patterns
Amethyst, calcite (orange), fluorite, labradorite, pyrite

Business matters
Amethyst, malachite

Calming
Agate, blue lace agate, amber, amethyst, aventurine (green), bloodstone, calcite (orange), carnelian, celestite, chrysocolla, fluorite, gold, goldstone, howlite, jade (nephrite), kyanite, larimar, lepidolite, moonstone, obsidian (black), petrified wood, quartz, quartz (rose), quartz (smoky), rhodonite, serpentine, sugilite, tourmaline

Centring
Calcite (orange), obsidian (black), quartz (smoky)

Challenges
Fluorite, garnet, obsidian (black)

Changes
Amethyst, calcite (orange), citrine, labradorite, lepidolite, malachite, rhodonite

Channelling
Amethyst, copper, fluorite, kyanite, quartz, sugilite

Clarity
Agate, blue lace agate, amber, amethyst, bloodstone, calcite (orange), celestite, chrysocolla, citrine, garnet, goldstone, hematite, jade (nephrite), kyanite, labradorite, lapis lazuli, larimar, malachite, obsidian (black), pyrite, quartz, rhodonite, selenite, serpentine, sodalite, sugilite, sunstone, tiger's eye, turquoise

Cleansing
Blue lace agate, moss agate, amber, brass, fluorite, garnet, labradorite, moonstone, obsidian (black), pyrite, quartz, quartz (rose), selenite, serpentine, silver, sodalite

Comfort
Aventurine (green), fluorite, jasper

Commitment
Garnet, tiger's eye, tourmaline

Communication
Blue lace agate, moss agate, celestite, chrysocolla, copper, fluorite, hematite, howlite, kyanite, larimar, moonstone, pyrite, quartz, silver, sodalite, turquoise

Concentration
Agate, bloodstone, carnelian, howlite, lapis lazuli, quartz

Confidence
Moss agate, calcite (orange), carnelian, citrine, copper, fluorite, garnet, goldstone, jade (nephrite), jasper, labradorite, lapis lazuli, moonstone, pyrite, rhodochrosite, rhodonite, sodalite, sugilite, unakite

Connection
Aventurine (green), bloodstone, howlite, kyanite, lepidolite, rhodochrosite, selenite, sodalite, sugilite

Contentment
Amethyst

Control
Carnelian, jasper (brown)

Co-operation
Copper, quartz (smoky)

Courage
Agate, blue lace agate, amethyst, aventurine (green), carnelian, chrysoprase, garnet, goldstone, howlite, jade (nephrite), labradorite, obsidian (black), petrified wood, sugilite, tiger's eye, tourmaline, unakite

Creativity
Blue lace agate, moss agate, amber, aventurine (green), bloodstone, calcite (orange), carnelian, citrine, garnet, goldstone, howlite, jade (nephrite), larimar, malachite, quartz (smoky), rhodochrosite, sodalite, tiger's eye, tourmaline

Deception (uncovering)
Bloodstone

Decisions
Aventurine (green), celestite, fluorite, hematite, kyanite, labradorite, lapis lazuli, larimar, lepidolite, petrified wood, pyrite, quartz, quartz (smoky), rhodonite, selenite, sodalite, sunstone, turquoise, unakite

Depression (Anti)
Moss agate, calcite (orange), carnelian, citrine, fluorite, garnet, labradorite, larimar, lepidolite, obsidian (black), quartz (rose), quartz (smoky), sunstone, turquoise

Determination
Calcite (orange), goldstone, jasper, obsidian (black), petrified wood, rhodochrosite, rhodonite, tiger's eye

Direction
Carnelian, goldstone

Divination
Moss agate, goldstone, hematite, lepidolite, moonstone, obsidian (black), pyrite, quartz, quartz (smoky), sodalite

Divine connection
Bloodstone, celestite, chrysocolla, copper, gold, larimar, quartz, selenite

Doubt (dispelling)
Carnelian, hematite

Dreams
Agate, aventurine (green), bloodstone, celestite, jade (nephrite), kyanite, lepidolite, moonstone, pebble, quartz, silver, sodalite

Emotions
Blue lace agate, moss agate, calcite (orange), chrysocolla, fluorite, goldstone, hematite, releasing, jade (nephrite), jasper (green), larimar, lepidolite, malachite, moonstone, obsidian (black), petrified wood, quartz, quartz (rose), quartz (smoky), rhodochrosite, rhodonite, selenite, serpentine, silver, sodalite, sugilite, sunstone, tourmaline, turquoise, unakite

Energy
Agate, amber, bloodstone, calcite (orange), chrysocolla, copper, garnet, gold, goldstone, jasper, labradorite, lapis lazuli, malachite, pyrite, quartz, rhodochrosite, rhodonite, silver, sunstone, turquoise

Fairy realm
Fluorite, pebble/hag stone, serpentine

Faith
Carnelian, goldstone

Fears (to alleviate)
Moss agate, calcite (orange), chrysocolla, citrine, garnet, jasper, larimar, malachite, petrified wood, quartz (rose), quartz (smoky), sodalite, sunstone, tiger's eye, tourmaline

Fertility
Moss agate, jade (nephrite), moonstone, pebble/hag stone, quartz (rose)

Finances
Moss agate, calcite (orange), hematite, jade (nephrite), malachite, pyrite, turquoise

Focus
Amethyst, howlite, jasper, labradorite, malachite, obsidian (black), pyrite, quartz, quartz (smoky), sugilite, tiger's eye

Friendship
Moss agate, jade (nephrite), larimar, sodalite, tourmaline, turquoise

Goodwill
Agate

Gossip (protection, deflection)
Garnet, quartz (rose)

Grounding
Amethyst, calcite (orange), carnelian, fluorite, hematite, jasper, kyanite, labradorite, obsidian (black), petrified wood, pyrite, quartz (rose), quartz (smoky), tiger's eye, tourmaline

Growth
Moss agate, kyanite, malachite, pyrite, quartz (rose), unakite

Guidance
Bloodstone, larimar, quartz (smoky)

Guilt (Removing)
Amethyst, chrysocolla

Happiness
Blue lace agate, moss agate, amethyst, aventurine (green), celestite, chrysoprase, citrine, gold, jasper, larimar, lepidolite, quartz (rose), rhodochrosite, rhodonite, sunstone, tourmaline, unakite

Harmony
Amber, carnelian, celestite, chrysocolla, copper, jade (nephrite), kyanite, lapis lazuli, larimar, lepidolite, moonstone, quartz, quartz (rose), rhodochrosite, rhodonite, sodalite, sunstone, tiger's eye, tourmaline, turquoise, unakite

Hate (protection, dispelling)
Carnelian

Healing
Blue lace agate, moss agate, amber, aventurine (green), bloodstone, brass, celestite, chrysoprase, citrine, fluorite, gold, hematite, jade (nephrite), jasper, kyanite, labradorite, larimar, malachite, moonstone, obsidian (black),pebble, pyrite, quartz, quartz (rose), rhodochrosite, selenite, silver, sugilite, sunstone, tiger's eye

Hidden knowledge
Amethyst

Honesty
Agate, carnelian, jasper

Hope
Moss agate, amethyst, lepidolite, moonstone

Illusions
Obsidian (black)

Imagination
Chrysoprase, fluorite, labradorite

Insight
Bloodstone, chrysocolla, labradorite, moonstone, petrified wood, quartz (smoky), sodalite, sugilite, tourmaline, turquoise

Inspiration
Amethyst, calcite (orange), garnet, howlite, labradorite, larimar, pyrite, quartz (rose), sugilite, sunstone

Intellect
Amber, aventurine (green), lapis lazuli

Intuition
Amethyst, bloodstone, chrysocolla, citrine, fluorite, labradorite, moonstone, quartz (rose), selenite, silver, sodalite, sunstone, turquoise

Invisibility
Bloodstone, jasper (black)

Jealousy (protection, dispelling)
Carnelian, labradorite, quartz (rose), quartz (smoky)

Journeying
Garnet, labradorite

Joy
Amber, citrine, rhodochrosite

Judgement
Amethyst

Justice
Blue lace agate, amethyst

Knowledge
Goldstone, lapis lazuli, sodalite

Leadership
Aventurine (green), calcite (orange), kyanite, lapis lazuli, petrified wood, sunstone

Legal issues
Amethyst, lapis lazuli

Learning
Gold, pyrite, quartz, sodalite

Longevity
Agate, blue lace agate, moss agate, jade (nephrite)

Love
Agate, moss agate, amber, aventurine (green), carnelian, celestite, chrysocolla, chrysoprase, copper, garnet, jade (nephrite), lapis lazuli, larimar, lepidolite, malachite, moonstone, quartz (rose), rhodochrosite, rhodonite, selenite, serpentine, silver, sodalite, sugilite, sunstone, turquoise, unakite

Luck
Moss agate, amethyst, aventurine (green), carnelian, chrysoprase,

copper, goldstone, jade (nephrite), kyanite, labradorite, lapis lazuli, lepidolite, obsidian (black), petrified wood, pyrite, quartz (rose), quartz (smoky), sunstone, tiger's eye, turquoise

Manifestation (as in manifesting goals and dreams...not bad spirits, although...)
Amber, fluorite, goldstone, hematite, jade (nephrite), jade (nephrite), lapis lazuli, malachite, pebble, pyrite, quartz, quartz (smoky), rhodochrosite, serpentine, silver

Marriage
Amber, chrysoprase

Meditation
Blue lace agate, amethyst, celestite, chrysocolla, fluorite, garnet, howlite, kyanite, labradorite, lapis lazuli, larimar, moonstone, obsidian (black), petrified wood, pyrite, quartz, quartz (smoky), selenite, serpentine, sodalite, turquoise

Memory
Agate, fluorite, lapis lazuli, pyrite

Money
Aventurine (green), bloodstone, calcite (orange), copper, goldstone, hematite, malachite, selenite, tiger's eye

Moon magic
Moonstone, silver

Motivation
Aventurine (green), carnelian, garnet, howlite, jasper, pyrite, quartz, tiger's eye, tourmaline

Mysticism
Bloodstone

Nature
Agate, moss agate, gold, quartz (smoky), serpentine, unakite

Negative energy (dispelling)
Bloodstone, carnelian, chrysocolla, chrysoprase, citrine, garnet, gold, goldstone, jasper (red/brick), lapis lazuli, pebble, quartz, quartz (smoky), rhodonite, serpentine, silver, tourmaline, turquoise

Nightmares (prevent)
Citrine, garnet, pebble/hag stone

Opportunities
Aventurine (green), calcite (orange), carnelian, lepidolite, malachite, sunstone, tiger's eye

Optimism
Blue lace agate, citrine, copper, goldstone, lepidolite, rhodonite, sunstone, tiger's eye

Organisation
Bloodstone, carnelian, fluorite, garnet, jasper, lapis lazuli, sodalite

Passion
Carnelian, garnet, quartz (rose), rhodonite, sugilite

Past life work
Bloodstone, fluorite, garnet, howlite, jade (nephrite), obsidian (black), petrified wood, turquoise

Patience
Blue lace agate, amber, amethyst, carnelian, chrysocolla, howlite, larimar, lepidolite, obsidian (black), petrified wood, rhodonite, silver, tiger's eye, tourmaline

Peace
Agate, blue lace agate, moss agate, amethyst, aventurine (green), calcite (orange), chrysocolla, celestite, fluorite, howlite, jade (nephrite), jasper, lapis lazuli, larimar, lepidolite, malachite, moonstone, quartz (rose), rhodochrosite, rhodonite, serpentine, silver, sodalite, sugilite, sunstone

Perception
Agate, aventurine (green), garnet, goldstone, pyrite

Perseverance
Calcite (orange), goldstone, labradorite, obsidian (black), petrified wood, pyrite, silver, sodalite, sunstone

Planning
Carnelian

Positive energy
Calcite (orange), copper

Potential
Calcite (orange), gold, goldstone, labradorite, rhodochrosite

Power
Amber, bloodstone, calcite (orange), fluorite, gold, jasper (grey), malachite, obsidian (black), pyrite, rhodochrosite, sunstone, tourmaline

Problems (Solving/dealing with)
Calcite (orange), hematite, lapis lazuli

Productivity
Calcite (orange), hematite

Prosperity
Blue lace agate, moss agate, chrysoprase, gold, jade (nephrite), jasper, malachite, moonstone, pyrite, quartz (rose), quartz (smoky), rhodochrosite, serpentine, silver, sunstone, tiger's eye, turquoise

Protection
Agate, blue lace agate, amber, amethyst, bloodstone, brass, calcite (orange), carnelian, chrysoprase, citrine, copper, fluorite, garnet, goldstone, hematite, jade (nephrite), jasper, labradorite, lapis lazuli, malachite, obsidian (black), pebble, pyrite, quartz, quartz (smoky), rhodonite, selenite, silver, serpentine, sugilite, sunstone, tiger's eye, tourmaline, tourmaline, turquoise

Psychic abilities
Amber, aventurine (green), chrysocolla, citrine, copper, jade (nephrite), kyanite, labradorite, lepidolite, malachite, moonstone, pyrite, quartz, rhodonite, selenite, silver, sodalite, sugilite, tiger's eye, turquoise

Psychic protection
Amethyst, carnelian, fluorite, lapis lazuli, selenite, serpentine

Purification
Amber, calcite (orange), brass, copper, fluorite, garnet, jade (nephrite), quartz, silver, turquoise

Releasing
Moss agate, calcite (orange), chrysocolla, chrysoprase, fluorite, howlite, jasper, lepidolite, malachite, obsidian (black), pyrite, quartz (smoky), rhodochrosite, rhodonite, sodalite, sugilite, tiger's eye, tourmaline, unakite

Relaxation
Blue lace agate, amethyst, fluorite, howlite, jasper, kyanite, labradorite, larimar, obsidian (black), quartz (smoky), rhodonite, tourmaline, turquoise

Renewal
Blue lace agate, moss agate, bloodstone, gold, jade (nephrite), lapis lazuli, malachite, rhodochrosite, rhodonite

Selfishness
Bloodstone, chrysoprase, howlite

Self confidence
Bloodstone, garnet, gold, labradorite, pyrite, rhodonite, sunstone, tiger's eye

Self esteem
Moss agate, citrine, copper, gold, hematite, quartz (rose), sodalite, sunstone

Self-worth
Carnelian, gold, tiger's eye

Sensuality
Amber, garnet, moonstone

Sexuality
Amber, garnet, quartz (rose)

Sleep
Agate, amethyst. Jasper (green), lapis lazuli, lepidolite, quartz (rose)

Soothing
Blue lace agate, amethyst, chrysocolla, labradorite, larimar, lepidolite, malachite, quartz (rose), rhodonite

Spirituality
Agate, blue lace agate, amethyst, bloodstone, celestite, chrysocolla, fluorite, garnet, gold, goldstone, jasper (grey), kyanite, labradorite, lapis lazuli, larimar, lepidolite, moonstone, obsidian (black), quartz, quartz (rose), rhodochrosite, rhodonite, selenite, silver, sugilite, tourmaline, turquoise, unakite

Spirit work
Celestite, garnet, jade (nephrite), obsidian (black), quartz, selenite

Stability
Moss agate, brass, carnelian, fluorite, hematite, jasper, kyanite, petrified wood, selenite, silver, sunstone, tourmaline, unakite

Stamina
Agate, carnelian, citrine

Strength
Agate, blue lace agate, moss agate, bloodstone, brass, chrysocolla, chrysoprase, garnet, hematite, howlite, labradorite, lepidolite, malachite, obsidian (black), petrified wood, pyrite, quartz, rhodochrosite, rhodonite, sugilite, sunstone, tiger's eye, tourmaline, unakite

Stress (To de-stress)
Agate, blue lace agate, moss agate, amber, celestite, citrine, gold, howlite, jasper, labradorite, lapis lazuli, lepidolite, malachite, obsidian (black), quartz (rose), rhodonite, sugilite, sunstone, turquoise

Structure
Fluorite

Success
Blue lace agate, moss agate, amber, amethyst, carnelian, chrysoprase, citrine, garnet, goldstone, labradorite, lapis lazuli, malachite, obsidian (black), petrified wood, pyrite, quartz (rose), selenite, serpentine, tiger's eye, unakite

Sun Magic
Amber, citrine, gold, pyrite, sunstone

Support
Blue lace agate, moss agate, aventurine (green), copper, fluorite, garnet, howlite, lepidolite, malachite, pyrite, quartz, tiger's eye, unakite

Transformation
Amethyst, chrysoprase, gold, jasper (red/brick), kyanite, labradorite, lepidolite, malachite, petrified wood, tourmaline, unakite

Travel
Blue lace agate, amethyst, malachite, moonstone, rhodonite, silver

Trust
Blue lace agate, moss agate, jasper, labradorite, lepidolite, quartz

(rose), rhodonite

Truth
Agate, blue lace agate, aventurine (green), bloodstone, carnelian, chrysoprase, garnet, howlite, jade (nephrite), kyanite, lapis lazuli, moonstone, obsidian (black), sodalite, sugilite

Understanding
Blue lace agate, amethyst, copper, gold, howlite, kyanite, lapis lazuli, larimar, sodalite, sugilite, tourmaline, turquoise

Uplifting
Blue lace agate, celestite, goldstone, jade (nephrite), larimar, lepidolite, moonstone, quartz, quartz (smoky), turquoise

Victory
Bloodstone

Visualisation
Aventurine (green)

Vitality
Amber, carnelian, kyanite, pyrite, rhodonite, tiger's eye

Wealth
Moss agate, bloodstone, brass, calcite (orange), citrine, gold, jade (nephrite), lapis lazuli, malachite, moonstone, obsidian (black), pyrite, silver, tiger's eye, turquoise, unakite

Wisdom
Agate, amber, chrysocolla, chrysoprase, gold, howlite, jade (nephrite), lapis lazuli, larimar, malachite, moonstone, petrified wood, pyrite, quartz, quartz (rose), sodalite, sugilite, turquoise

Wishes

Amber, moonstone, quartz (smoky)

Elements

Each crystal is associated with one of the elements dependent on its characteristics, magical properties and often its colour. I have listed below the crystals within this book into their elements, but as always trust your intuition. If you want to use a piece of bloodstone for water, go with it – just be certain that it feels right to you.

Earth

Agate (moss), bloodstone, calcite (orange), chrysoprase, goldstone, hematite, howlite, jasper (green), malachite, obsidian (black), pebble, petrified wood, quartz (rose), quartz (smoky), tiger's eye, tourmaline (green, black), turquoise

Air

Aventurine (green), celestite, fluorite, jasper (brown), jasper (grey)

Fire

Agate, amber, bloodstone, carnelian, citrine, garnet, gold, goldstone, hematite, jasper (red/brick), jasper (black), larimar, obsidian (black), pyrite, quartz, rhodochrosite, rhodonite, serpentine, sunstone, tiger's eye, tourmaline (watermelon, red), unakite

Water

Agate (blue lace), amethyst, celestite, chrysocolla, copper, fluorite, jade, kyanite (blue), labradorite, lapis lazuli, larimar, lepidolite, moonstone, obsidian (black), pebble, quartz, quartz (rose), selenite, silver, sodalite, sugilite, tourmaline (pink, blue, watermelon), unakite

Spirit/Ether
Amber, larimar, petrified wood

Planets

Each crystal is associated with one of the planets dependent on its characteristics, magical properties and often its colour. I have listed below the crystals within this book into the planets they correspond to, but as always trust your intuition. If you want to use a piece of howlite to represent Jupiter, go with it – just be certain that it feels right to you.

Earth
Howlite, labradorite, pebble, petrified wood

Jupiter
Amethyst, citrine, goldstone, kyanite (blue), lapis lazuli, lepidolite, obsidian (black), quartz (smoky), rhodochrosite, selenite, sodalite, sugilite

Mars
Aventurine (green), bloodstone, garnet, jasper (red/brick), kyanite (blue), pyrite, rhodochrosite, rhodonite, tourmaline, unakite

Mercury
Agate, agate (blue lace), aventurine (green), jasper (brown), sugilite

Moon
Agate (moss), howlite, jasper (grey), labradorite, moonstone, silver, quartz, quartz (rose)

Neptune
Amethyst, celestite, fluorite, jade, larimar, lepidolite, turquoise

Pluto
Unakite

Saturn
Hematite, obsidian (black), quartz (smoky), serpentine

Sun
Amber, calcite (orange), carnelian, citrine, gold, petrified wood, pyrite, quartz, sunstone, tiger's eye

Uranus
Jasper (black), labradorite

Venus
Celestite, chrysocolla, chrysoprase, copper, goldstone, jade, jasper (green), kyanite (blue), lapis lazuli, malachite, quartz (rose), rhodonite, selenite, sodalite, tourmaline, turquoise, unakite

Birthstone and Zodiac lists are towards the front of this book.

Sparkly endings

Working with crystals in magic can be extremely rewarding. The magic that can be created with just one small tumble stone is astounding. I know I say it a lot, but... trust your intuition when working with your stones, the magic is within.

**MOON
BOOKS**

PAGANISM & SHAMANISM

What is Paganism? A religion, a spirituality, an alternative
belief system, nature worship? You can find support for all these
definitions (and many more) in dictionaries, encyclopaedias, and
text books of religion, but subscribe to any one and the truth will
evade you. Above all Paganism is a creative pursuit, an encounter
with reality, an exploration of meaning and an expression of the
soul. Druids, Heathens, Wiccans and others, all contribute their
insights and literary riches to the Pagan tradition. Moon Books
invites you to begin or to deepen your own encounter, right here,
right now.
If you have enjoyed this book, why not tell other readers by
posting a review on your preferred book site.

Recent bestsellers from Moon Books are:

Journey to the Dark Goddess
How to Return to Your Soul
Jane Meredith
Discover the powerful secrets of the Dark Goddess and
transform your depression, grief and pain into healing
and integration.
Paperback: 978-1-84694-677-6 ebook: 978-1-78099-223-5

Shamanic Reiki
Expanded Ways of Working with Universal Life Force Energy
Llyn Roberts, Robert Levy
Shamanism and Reiki are each powerful ways of healing; together,
their power multiplies. *Shamanic Reiki* introduces techniques to
help healers and Reiki practitioners tap ancient healing wisdom.
Paperback: 978-1-84694-037-8 ebook: 978-1-84694-650-9

Pagan Portals – The Awen Alone
Walking the Path of the Solitary Druid
Joanna van der Hoeven
An introductory guide for the solitary Druid, *The Awen Alone* will
accompany you as you explore, and seek out your own place
within the natural world.
Paperback: 978-1-78279-547-6 ebook: 978-1-78279-546-9

A Kitchen Witch's World of Magical Herbs & Plants
Rachel Patterson
A journey into the magical world of herbs and plants, filled with
magical uses, folklore, history and practical magic. By popular
writer, blogger and kitchen witch, Tansy Firedragon.
Paperback: 978-1-78279-621-3 ebook: 978-1-78279-620-6

Medicine for the Soul
The Complete Book of Shamanic Healing
Ross Heaven
All you will ever need to know about shamanic healing and how to
become your own shaman...
Paperback: 978-1-78099-419-2 ebook: 978-1-78099-420-8

Shaman Pathways – The Druid Shaman
Exploring the Celtic Otherworld
Danu Forest
A practical guide to Celtic shamanism with exercises and
techniques as well as traditional lore for exploring the Celtic
Otherworld.
Paperback: 978-1-78099-615-8 ebook: 978-1-78099-616-5

Traditional Witchcraft for the Woods and Forests
A Witch's Guide to the Woodland with Guided Meditations and
Pathworking
Mélusine Draco
A Witch's guide to walking alone in the woods, with guided
meditations and pathworking.
Paperback: 978-1-84694-803-9 ebook: 978-1-84694-804-6

Wild Earth, Wild Soul
A Manual for an Ecstatic Culture
Bill Pfeiffer
Imagine a nature-based culture so alive and so connected,
spreading like wildfire. This book is the first flame...
Paperback: 978-1-78099-187-0 ebook: 978-1-78099-188-7

Naming the Goddess
Trevor Greenfield
Naming the Goddess is written by over eighty adherents and
scholars of Goddess and Goddess Spirituality.
Paperback: 978-1-78279-476-9 ebook: 978-1-78279-475-2

Shapeshifting into Higher Consciousness
Heal and Transform Yourself and Our World with Ancient
Shamanic and Modern Methods
Llyn Roberts
Ancient and modern methods that you can use every day to
transform yourself and make a positive difference in the world.
Paperback: 978-1-84694-843-5 ebook: 978-1-84694-844-2

Readers of ebooks can buy or view any of these bestsellers by
clicking on the live link in the title. Most titles are published in
paperback and as an ebook. Paperbacks are available in traditional
bookshops. Both print and ebook formats are available online.

Find more titles and sign up to our readers' newsletter at
http://www.johnhuntpublishing.com/paganism
Follow us on Facebook at https://www.facebook.com/MoonBooks
and Twitter at https://twitter.com/MoonBooksJHP